TITLES AND FIRST LINES

ACKNOWLEDGMENTS

- **Bob Griggs:** introduced me to the guitar.
- **David Hughes:** my one and only guitar teacher. Didn't take a dime – and sold me his guitar.
- **Les Paul:** inspired me to play.
- **Chet Atkins:** inspired me to play like him.
- **Lairy Wood:** revealed harmonic melody's secret.
- **David Chugg:** bravely hired me to teach guitar at University level.
- **Thousands** of college students who have suffered through the years of development leading to this book.
- Sons, **John** and **Matthew Kimball**: for providing me with the Mac and PC computers.
- **Don Bird:** his software gift of AutoCad made it all possible.
- **Adrian Baird:** instructed me how to create the thousands of guitar symbols in the computer.
- Daughters, **Cynthia** and **Janine**: played the hymns into the computer from the piano.

- Daughter, **Suzanne:** edited my lesson book.*
- **other family members**: who have cheered me on.
- **And, most of all,** my dear wife, **Gloria**, whose gentle urging has led to this collection of our beloved gospel songs, written for the first time in *GuitarPerfect™ Full-Picture Harmonic Melody*. Her patience and advice over the years has sustained me and made it all possible.

May *God Be With You 'Til We Meet Again*, playing these wonderful and beautiful hymns.

Newel Kimball

* The "Kimball Harmonic Melody Guitar Method" is a complete course on music and guitar theory. $25.00 US. Order from: *Oxbow P   PO Box 112, Victor, ID 83455 Phone 208-787-*

ACCOMPANIMENT CHORDS AND CHORD FAMILIES

Five of the 12 possible *Chord Family* charts are shown here for the easiest guitar keys, namely **A, D, E, C,** and **G.** The chords as shown may be used as accompaniment chords, with picking patterns from the inside back cover. Each of the five charts show a full-picture fret-board of the *key*, or *tonic* chord of the family, along with 11 other chords that have a traditional relationship. Each chart shows three columns, and four rows of fretboards. The chords are arranged this way for visual simplicity, beginning with the **tonic**, (2nd row-circled). The next most-used chord is at tonic's right (*dominant 7th*), and the next most used chord is at tonic's left (**sub-dominant**). These 2nd-row chords are always *major*. On the third row are three chords that are called *relative minors*. The first row contains three chords by the same alphabetical name as those on the second row, and are called *parallel minors*. The fourth row contains three chords by the same alphabetical name as those on the third row, and are called *parallel majors*. Each of the 12 keys (or charts) has the same layout of related chords. Most of the music we listen to (and all of the hymns) use these relational charts for the chord choices of a song. So... **how** did these relationships come about?

While the word "**octave**" means "eight", there have actually always been 12 notes in an "octave"(counting both the *white* and *black* keys) The reason for this mis-naming is due to the fact that the ancients only used (and numbered) a specific seven of the 12 notes for their music. These original notes can be thought of as the **white keys** of the piano. The "**black**" keys (*sharps* and/or *flats*) were not sung or played. In fact, ancient instruments did not include the five missing notes. Since there are seven original notes in an octave (not counting the eighth note with the same name as the first), a different *scale* begins on each of the seven notes–three **major** (bright), three **minor** (gloomy) and one **diminished** (a mixture of both). This system of melody creation was called *modes*, meaning "**method**"–for writing melodies.

Three harmonizing notes, called "**triads**", are to be found within each of the seven different scales. As in the scales, there are three **major triads**, three **minor triads**, and one **diminished triad** (seldom used). Songs may use either major triads as the main basis, with the minor triads as "**relatives**", or minor triads can dominate.

The older hymns used the original six-chord grouping, but with the eventual inclusion of the "black" keys, **major** triads could be played as minor, and **minor** triads played as major, (called **parallel chords**), adding six more chords to the original six–and thus the **12-Chord Family** often used for modern hymns and songs.

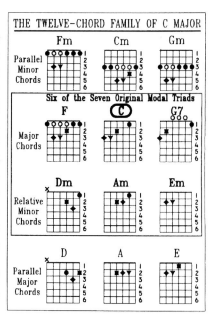

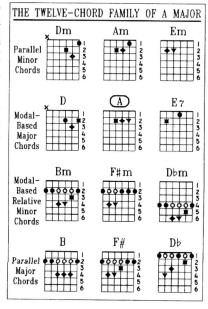

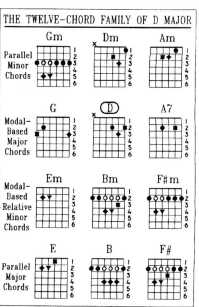

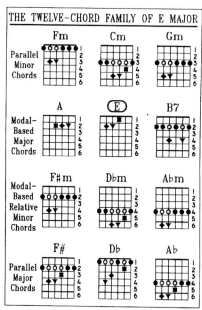

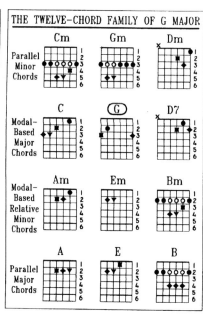

The Hymns

A POOR WAYFARING MAN OF GRIEF

Words: James Montgomery   Kimball GuitarPerfect arr.© 2003   Music: George Coles

A POOR WAYFARING MAN OF GRIEF (cont.)

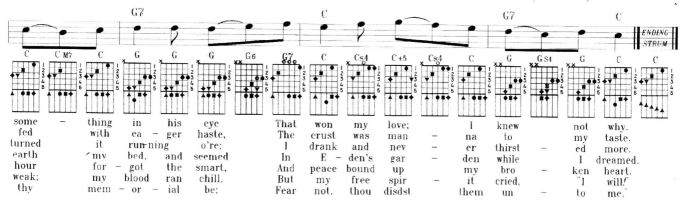

ABIDE WITH ME

Words: Henry F. Lyte

Kimball GuitarPerfect arr.© 2003

Music: William H. Monk

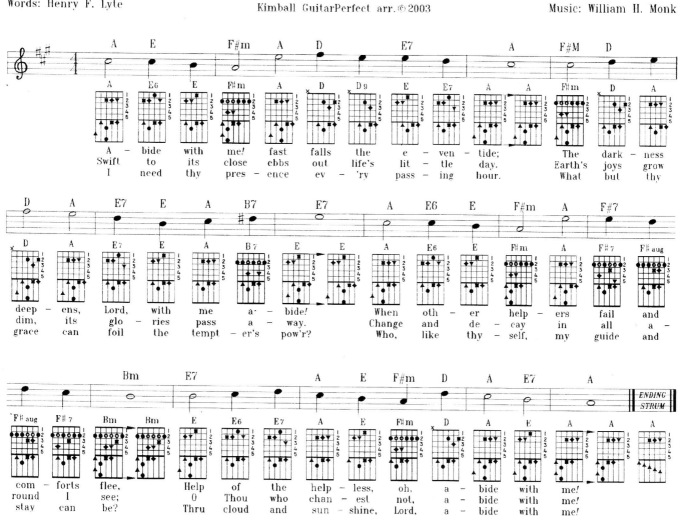

ABIDE WITH ME, 'TIS EVENTIDE

Words: Lowrie M. Hoffard

Kimball GuitarPerfect arr.© 2003

Music: Harrison Millard

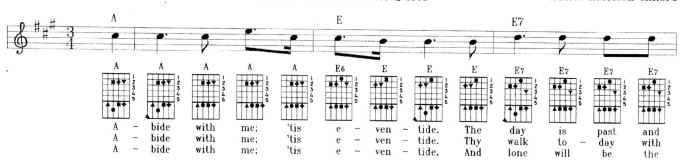

A - bide with me; 'tis e - ven - tide. The day is past and
A - bide with me; 'tis e - ven - tide. Thy walk to day with
A - bide with me; 'tis e - ven - tide, And lone will be the

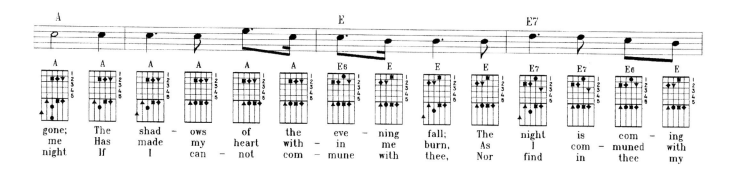

gone; The shad - ows of the eve - ning fall; The night is com - ing
me; Has made I my can heart not with com - mune in me with thee, The As night I com - muned with
night If made my can not com - mune with thee, burn, Nor find in thee my

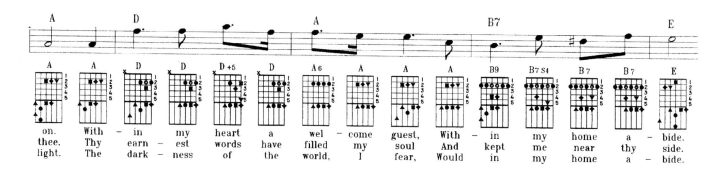

on. With Thy - in my heart words have fall - come my guest, With - in my home a - bide.
thee. The earn - est of a wel - come soul fear, And kept in me near thy side.
light. The dark - ness of the world, I Would in my home a - bide.

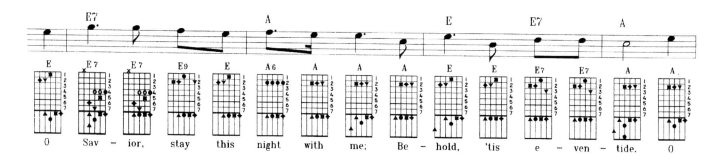

O Sav - ior, stay this night with me; Be - hold, 'tis e - ven - tide. O

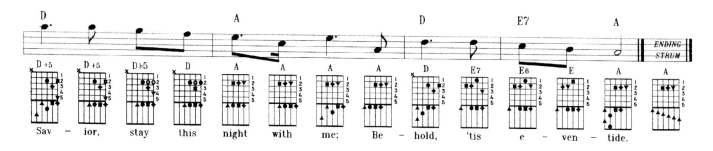

Sav - ior, stay this night with me; Be - hold, 'tis e - ven - tide.

A MIGHTY FORTRESS IS OUR GOD

Words: Martin Luther   Kimball GuitarPerfect arr.© 2003   Music: Attr. to Martin Luther

4

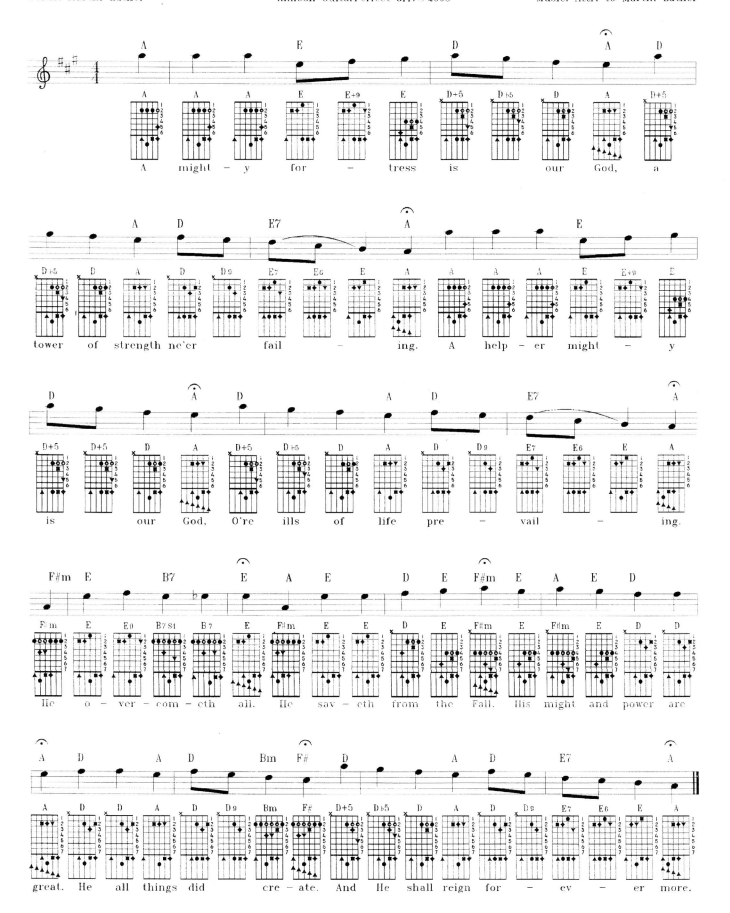

AMAZING GRACE

Kimball GuitarPerfect arr. ©2003

Words: John Newton

Music: John Newton

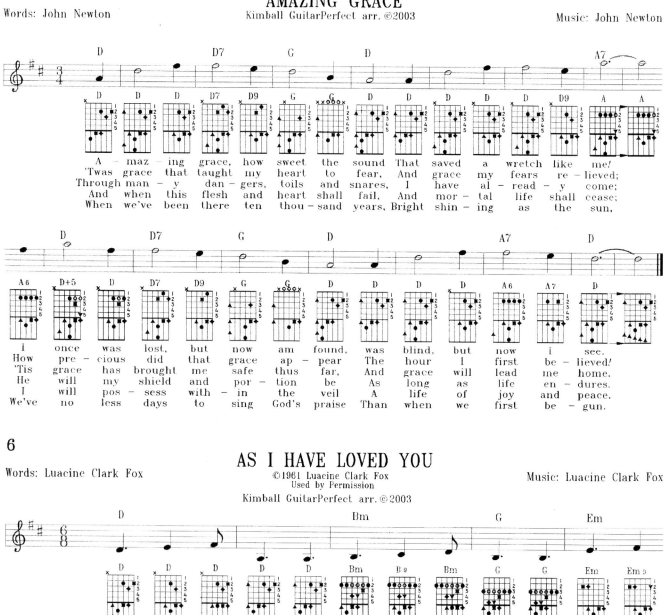

A - maz - ing grace, how sweet the sound That saved a wretch like me!
'Twas grace that taught my heart to fear, And grace my fears re - lieved;
Through man - y dan - gers, toils and snares, I have al - read - y come;
And when this flesh and heart shall fail, And mor - tal life shall cease;
When we've been there ten thou - sand years, Bright shin - ing as the sun,

i once was lost, but now am found, was blind, but now i see.
How pre - cious did that grace ap - pear The hour I first be - lieved!
'Tis grace has brought me safe thus far, And grace will lead me home.
He will my shield and por - tion be As long as life en - dures.
I will pos - sess with - in the veil A life of joy and peace.
We've no less days to sing God's praise Than when we first be - gun.

AS I HAVE LOVED YOU

©1961 Luacine Clark Fox
Used by Permission

Kimball GuitarPerfect arr. ©2003

Words: Luacine Clark Fox

Music: Luacine Clark Fox

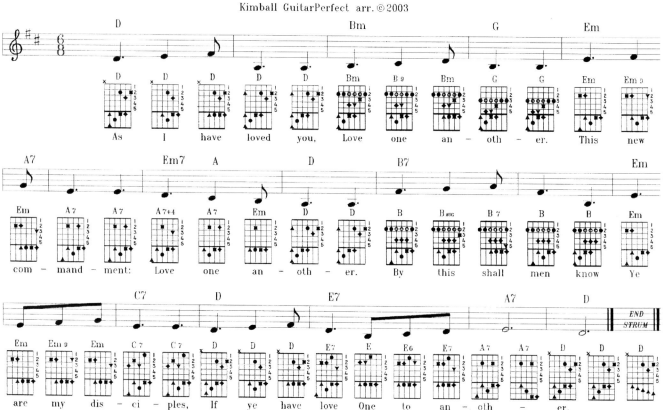

As I have loved you, Love one an - oth - er. This new

com - mand - ment: Love one an - oth - er. By this shall men know Ye

are my dis - ci - ples, If ye have love One to an - oth - er.

END STRUM

BE STILL, MY SOUL

Kimball GuitarPerfect arr. © 2003

Words: Katherine Von Schlegel
Trans. by Jane Borthwick

Music: Jean Sebelius
From "*Finlandia*"

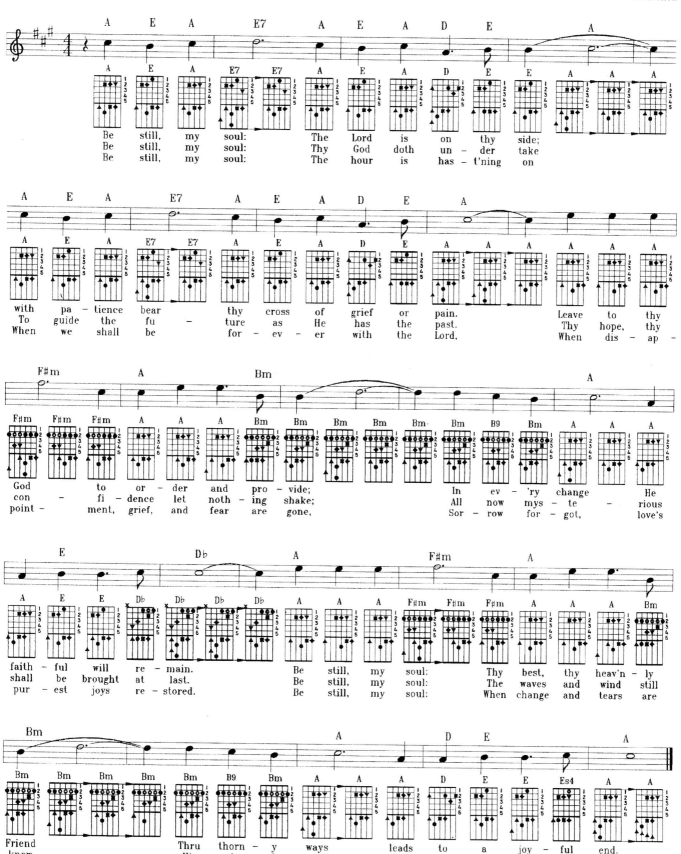

BRIGHTLY BEAMS OUR FATHER'S MERCY

Words & Music: Philip Paul Bliss   Kimball GuitarPerfect arr.© 2003

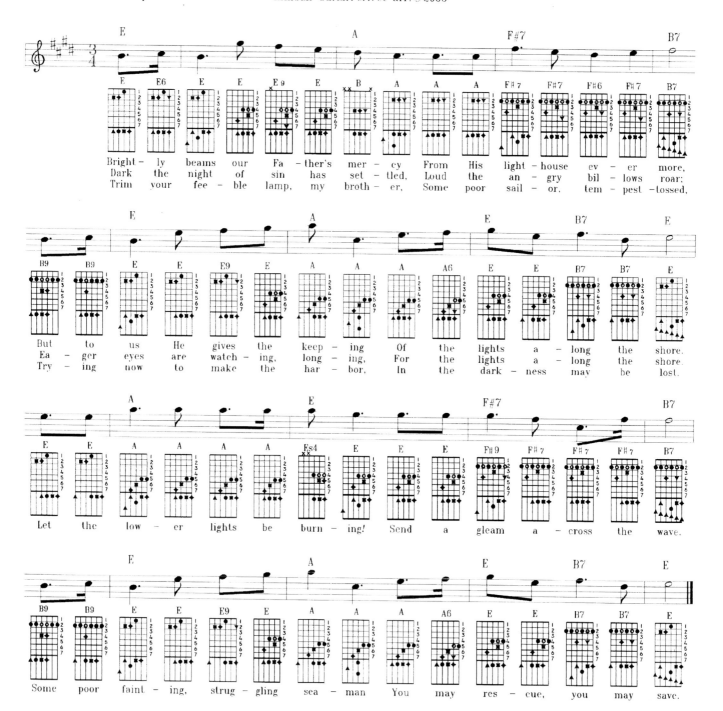

BRINGING IN THE SHEAVES

Words: Knowles Shaw

Kimball GuitarPerfect arr.© 2003

Music: George A. Minor

Sow — ing in the morn — ing, sow — ing seeds of kind — ness,
Sow — ing in the sun — shine, sow — ing in the shad — ows,
Go — ing forth with weep — ing, sow — ing for the Mas — ter,

Sow — ing in the noon — tide and the dew — y eve, Wait — ing for the har — vest
Fear — ing nei — ther clowds nor win — ter's chill — ing breeze, By and by the har — vest
Tho' the loss sus — tained our spir — it of — ten grieves, When our weep — ing's o — ver

and the time of reap — ing, We shall come re — joic — ing bring — ing in the sheaves.
and the la — bor end — ed. We shall come re — joic — ing bring — ing in the sheaves.
He will bid us wel — come. We shall come re — joic — ing bring — ing in the sheaves.

Bring — ing in the sheaves, Bring — ing in the sheaves, We shall come re — joic — ing

Bring — ing in the sheaves. bring — ing in the sheaves. bring — ing in the sheaves,

We shall come re — joic — ing bring — ing in the sheaves.

ENDING STRUM

CHOOSE THE RIGHT

Words: Joseph L. Townsend

Kimball GuitarPerfect arr.© 2003

Music: Henry A. Tuckett

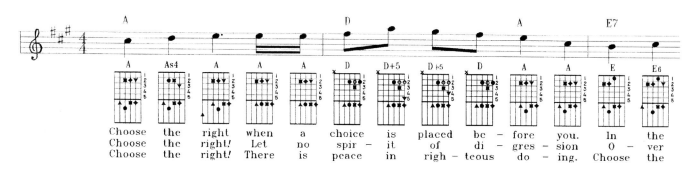

Choose the right when a choice is placed be — fore you. In the
Choose the right! Let no spir — it of di — gres — sion O — ver
Choose the right! There is peace in righ — teous do — ing. Choose the

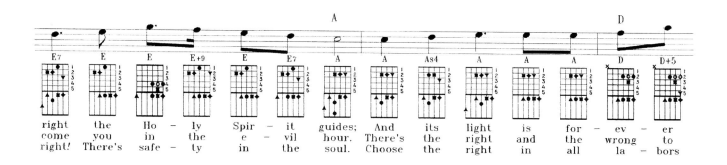

right the Ho — ly Spir — it guides; And its light is for — ev — er
come you in the e — vil hour. There's the right in all la — bors
right! There's safe — ty in the soul. Choose the right and wrong to

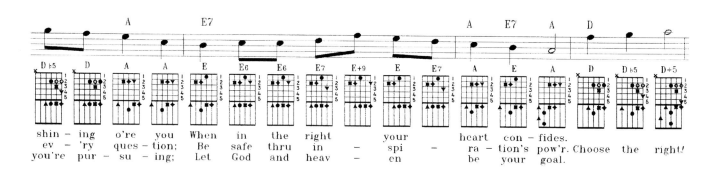

shin — ing o're you When in the right your heart con — fides.
ev — 'ry ques — tion; Be safe thru in — your spi — ra — tion's pow'r. Choose the right!
you're pur — su — ing; Let God and heav — en be your goal.

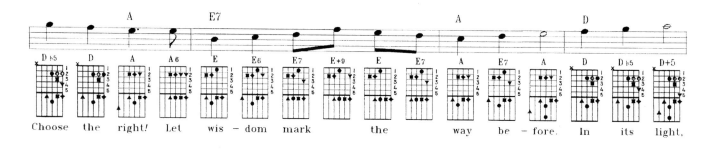

Choose the right! Let wis — dom mark the way be — fore. In its light,

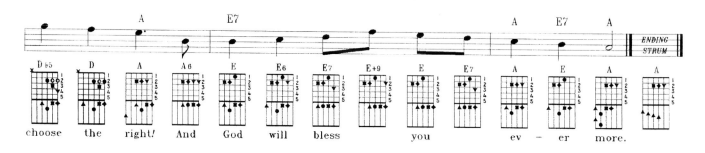

ENDING STRUM

choose the right! And God will bless you ev — er more.

COME, FOLLOW ME

Words: John Nicholson

Kimball GuitarPerfect arr. © 2003

Music: Samuel McBurney

DO WHAT IS RIGHT

Anon., The Psalms of Life, Boston, 1857   Kimball GuitarPerfect arr.© 2003   Music: E. Kiallmark

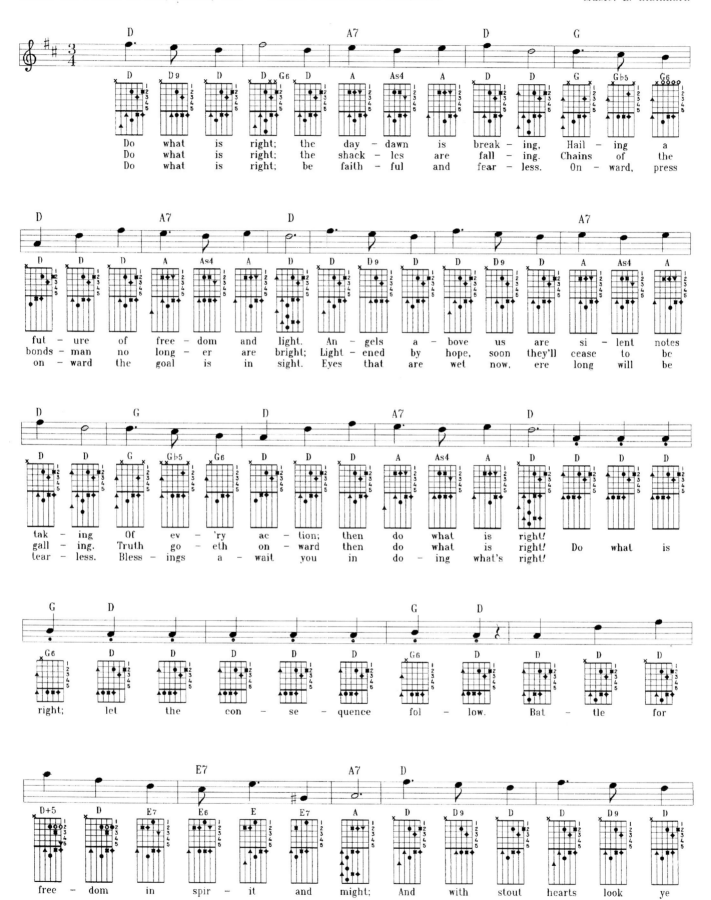

COME UNTO JESUS

Words and Music: Orson Pratt Huish

Kimball GuitarPerfect arr.© 2003

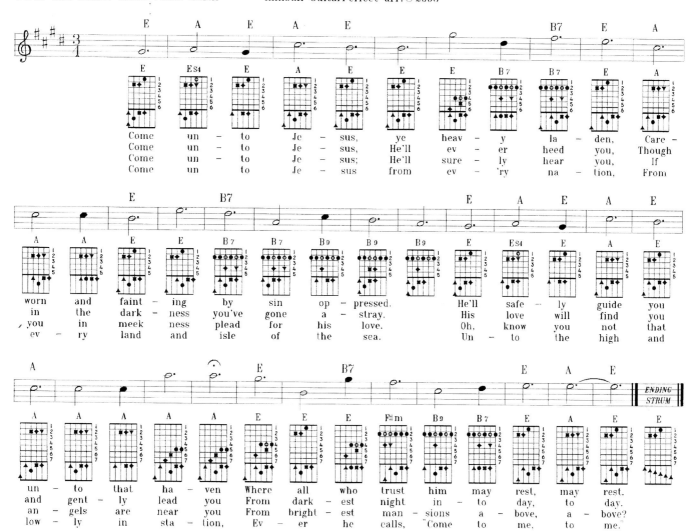

DO WHAT IS RIGHT

Anon., The Psalms of Life, Boston, 1857   Kimball GuitarPerfect arr.© 2003   Music: E. Kiallmark

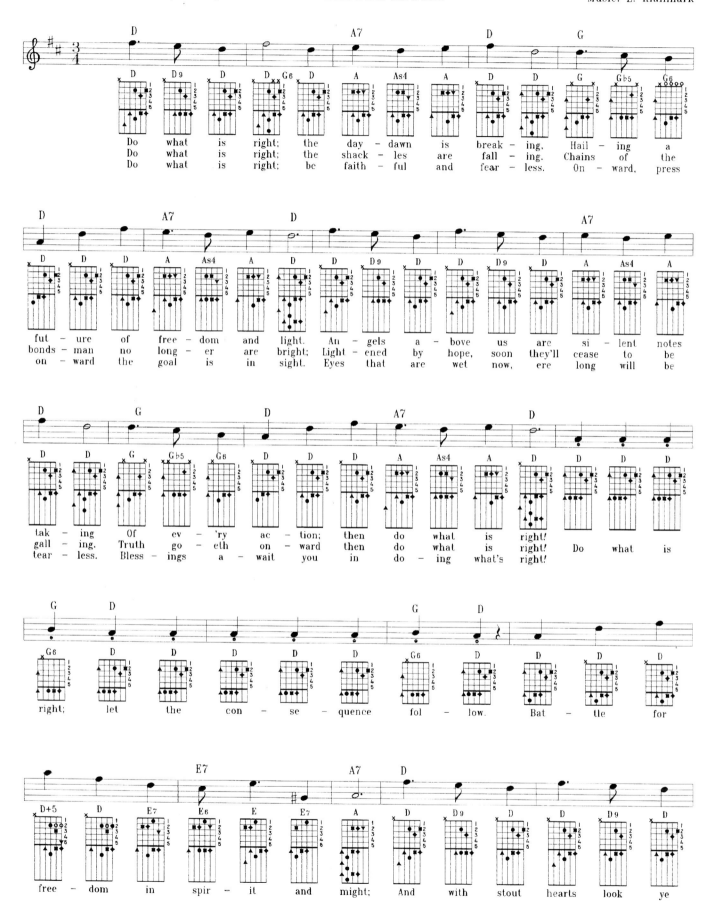

DO WHAT IS RIGHT (cont.)

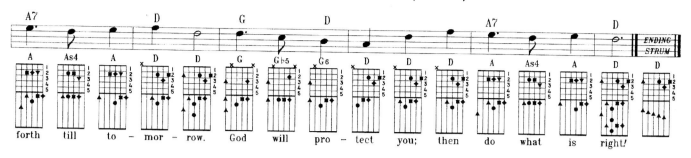

COME, THOU ALMIGHTY KING

Words: Anonymous

Kimball GuitarPerfect arr.© 2003

Music: Felice De Giardini

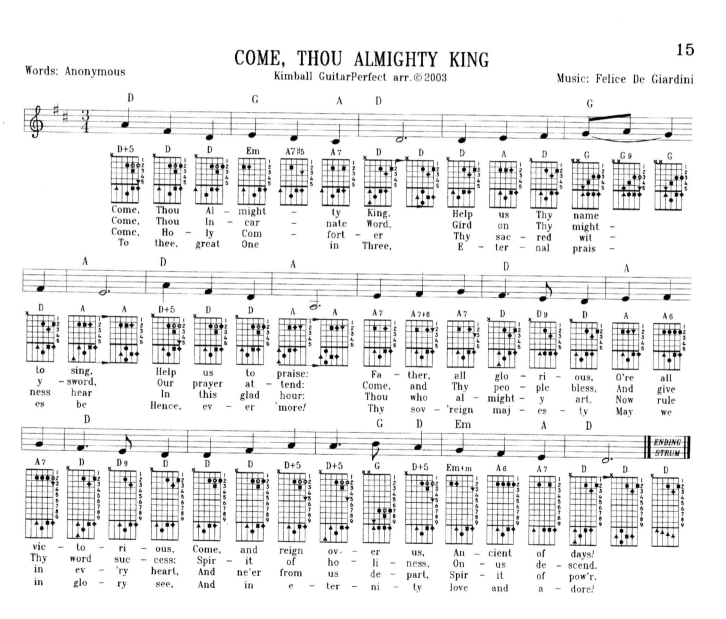

DEAR TO THE HEART OF THE SHEPHERD

Words: Mary B. Wingate

Kimball GuitarPerfect arr.© 2003

Music: William J. Kirkpatrick

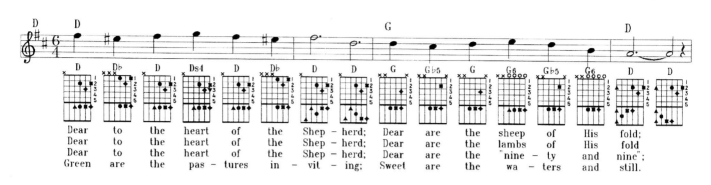

Dear to the heart of the Shep – herd; Dear are the sheep of His fold;
Dear to the heart of the Shep – herd; Dear are the lambs of His fold;
Green are the pas – tures in – vit – ing; Sweet are the wa – ters and still.

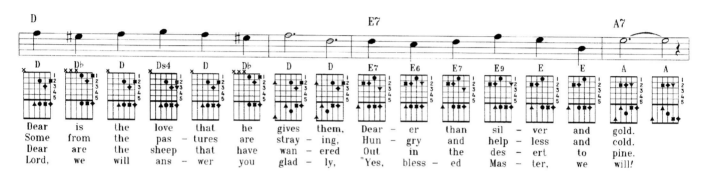

Dear is the love that he gives them, Dear – er than sil – ver and gold.
Some from the pas – tures are stray – ing, Hun – gry and help – less and cold.
Dear are the sheep that have wan – ered Out in the des – ert to pine.
Lord, we will ans – wer you glad – ly, "Yes, bless – ed Mas – ter, we will!

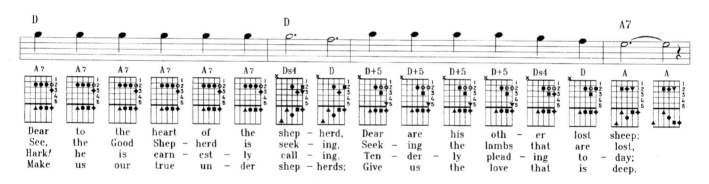

Dear to the heart of the shep – herd, Dear are his oth – er lost sheep;
See, the Good Shep – herd is seek – ing, Seek – ing the lambs that are lost,
Hark! he is earn – est – ly call – ing, Ten – der – ly plead – ing to – day;
Make us our true un – der shep – herds; Give us the love that is deep.

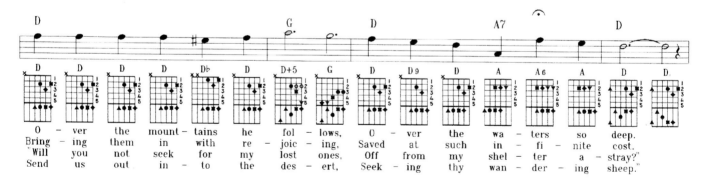

O – ver the mount – tains he fol – lows, O – ver the wa – ters so deep.
Bring – ing them in with re – joic – ing, Saved at such in – fi – nite cost.
"Will you not seek with for my lost ones, Off from my shel – ter a – stray?"
Send us out in – to the des – ert, Seek – ing thy wan – der – ing sheep."

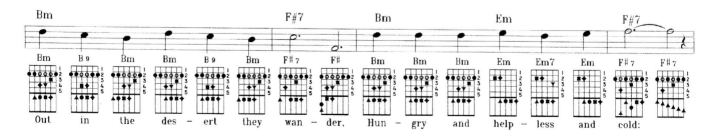

Out in the des – ert they wan – der, Hun – gry and help – less and cold:

DEAR TO THE HEART OF THE SHEPHERD (cont.)

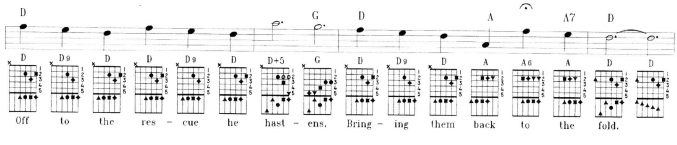

Off to the res — cue he hast — ens, Bring — ing them back to the fold.

GOD IS LOVE

Words: Thomas R. Taylor Kimball GuitarPerfect arr.© 2003 Music:Thomas C. Griggs

Earth with her ten thou — sand flow'rs, Air with all its
Sounds a — mong the vails and ly hills In the woods and
All the hopes that sweet — start From the foun — tain

beams and show'rs, Heav — en's in — fi — nite ex — pance,
by the rills Of the breeze and of the bird,
of the heart, All the bliss that ev — er comes

Sea's re — splen — dent coun — te — nance All a — round and
by the gen — tle m,ur — mur stirred Sac — red songs, be
To our earth — ly hu — man homes, All the voic — es

all a — bove Bear this rec — cord: God is love.
neath, a — bove, Have this one chor — us: God is love.
from a — bove Sweet — ly whis — per: God is love.

ENDING STRUM

DID YOU THINK TO PRAY?

Words: Mary A. Pepper Kidder

Kimball GuitarPerfect arr.© 2003

Music: William O. Perkins

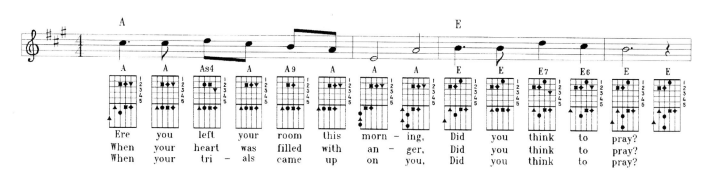

Ere you left your room this morn – ing, Did you think to pray?
When your heart was filled with an – ger, Did you think to pray?
When your tri – als came up on you, Did you think to pray?

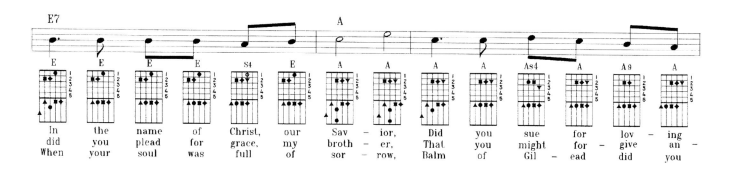

In the name of Christ, our Sav – ior, Did you sue for lov – ing
did you plead for grace, my broth – er, That you might for – give an –
When your soul was full of sor – row, Balm of Gil – ead did you

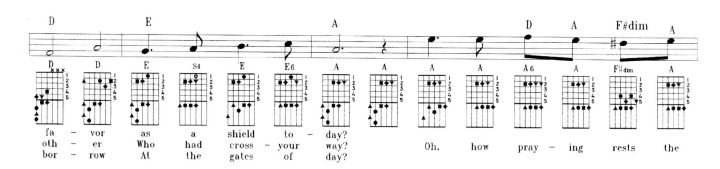

fa – vor as a shield to – day?
oth – er Who had the cross – your way? Oh, how pray – ing rests the
bor – row At the gates of day?

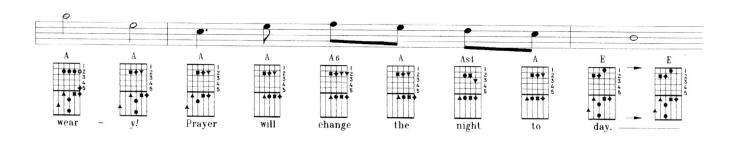

wear – y! Prayer will change the night to day.

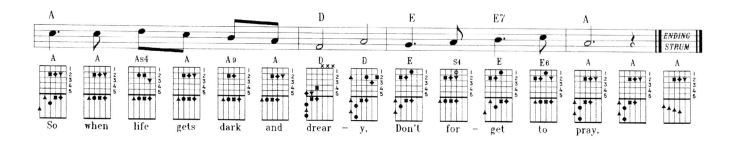

So when life gets dark and drear – y, Don't for – get to pray.

GOD BE WITH YOU TILL WE MEET AGAIN

Jeremiah E. Rankin, 1828-1904   Kimball GuitarPerfect arr. ©2002   William G. Tomer, 1833-1896

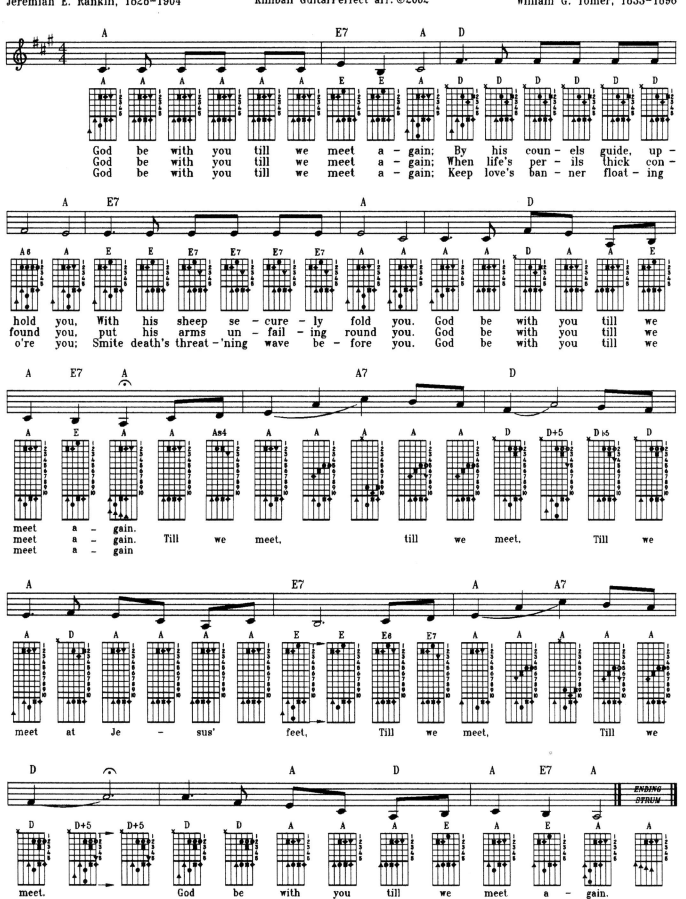

GOD BE WITH YOU TILL WE MEET AGAIN

Words: Jeremiah E. Rankin

Kimball GuitarPerfect arr.© 2003

Music: William G. Tomer

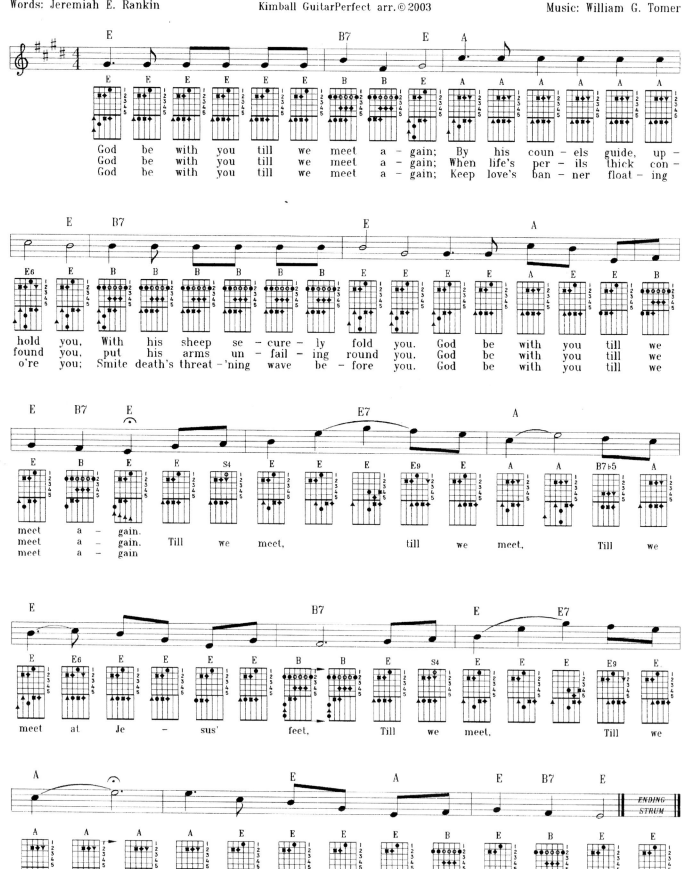

HE DIED, THE GREAT REDEEMER DIED

Kimball GuitarPerfect arr. © 2003

Words: Isaac Watts

Music: George Careless

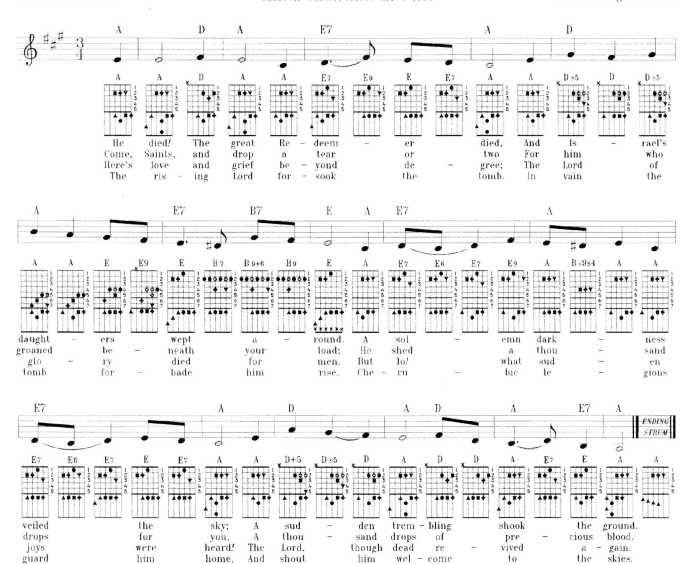

He died! The great Re — deem — er died, And Is — rael's
Come, Saints, love and drop a tear or two For him who
Here's ris — ing Lord be — yond de — gree; The Lord of the
The and grief for — sook the tomb. In vain the

daught — ers wept — a — round. A sol — emn dark — ness
groaned be — neath your load; He shed a thou — sand
glo — ry died for men. But lo! what sud — en
tomb for bade him rise. Che — ru — bic le — gions

veiled the sky; A sud — den trem — bling shook the ground.
drops for you, A thou sand drops of pre — cious blood.
joys were heard! The Lord, sand dead re — vived a — gain.
guard him home, And shout him wel — come to the skies.

ENDING STRUM

HOLY, HOLY, HOLY

Words: Reginald Heber

Kimball GuitarPerfect arr.©2003

Music: John B. Dykes

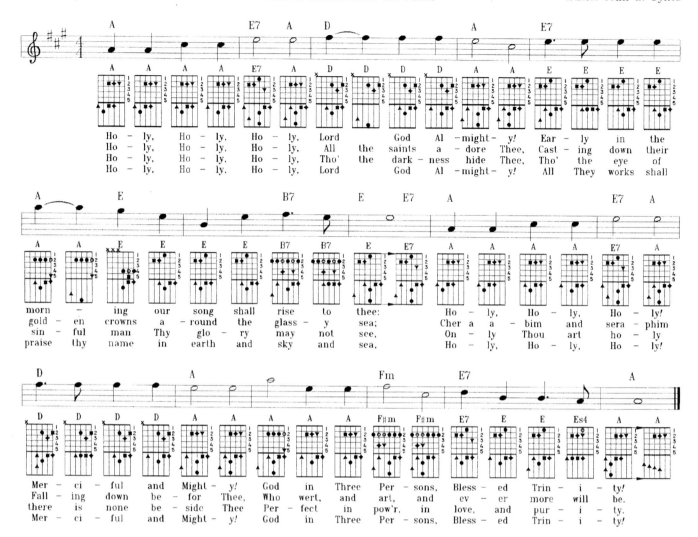

Ho - ly, Ho - ly, Ho - ly, Lord God Al - might - y! Ear - ly in the
Ho - ly, Ho - ly, Ho - ly, All the saints a - dore Thee, Cast - ing down their
Ho - ly, Ho - ly, Ho - ly, Tho' the dark - ness hide Thee, Tho' the eye of
Ho - ly, Ho - ly, Ho - ly, Lord God Al - might - y! All They works shall

morn — ing our song shall rise to thee: Ho - ly, Ho - ly, Ho - ly!
gold - en crowns a - round the glass - y sea; Cher a a - bim and sera - phim
sin - ful man Thy glo - ry may not see, On - ly Thou art ho - ly
praise thy name in earth and sky and sea, Ho - ly, Ho - ly, Ho - ly!

Mer - ci - ful and Might - y! God in Three Per - sons, Bless - ed Trin - i - ty!
Fall - ing down be - for Thee, Who wert, and art, and ev - er more will be.
there is none be - side Thee Per - fect in pow'r, in love, and pur - i - ty.
Mer - ci - ful and Might - y! God in Three Per - sons, Bless - ed Trin - i - ty!

HOW FIRM A FOUNDATION

Words: Attr. to Robert Keen

Kimball GuitarPerfect arr.© 2003

Music: Anonymous

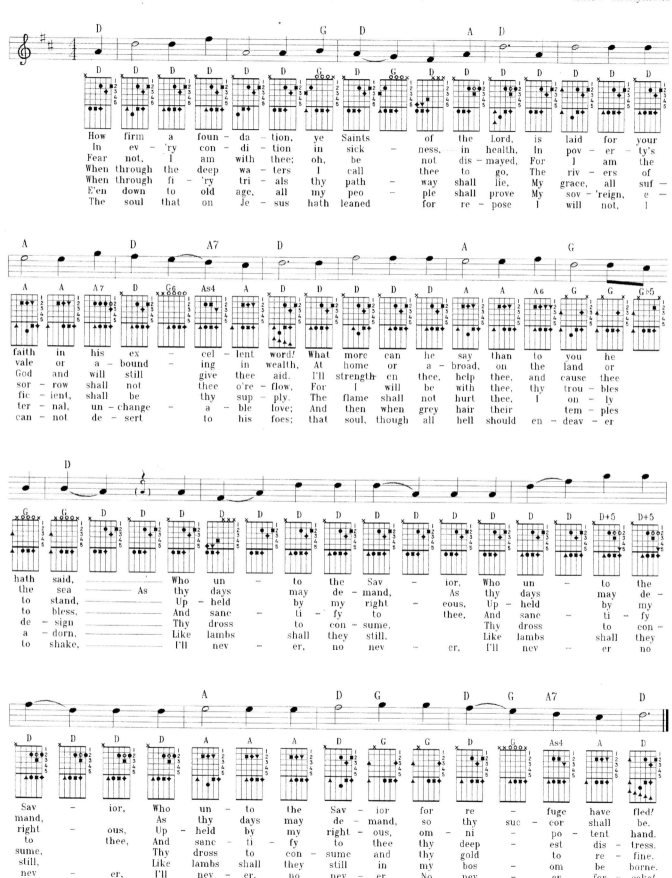

HOW GENTLE GOD'S COMMANDS

Kimball GuitarPerfect arr.© 2003

Words: Philip Doddridge

Music: Johan G. Nageli

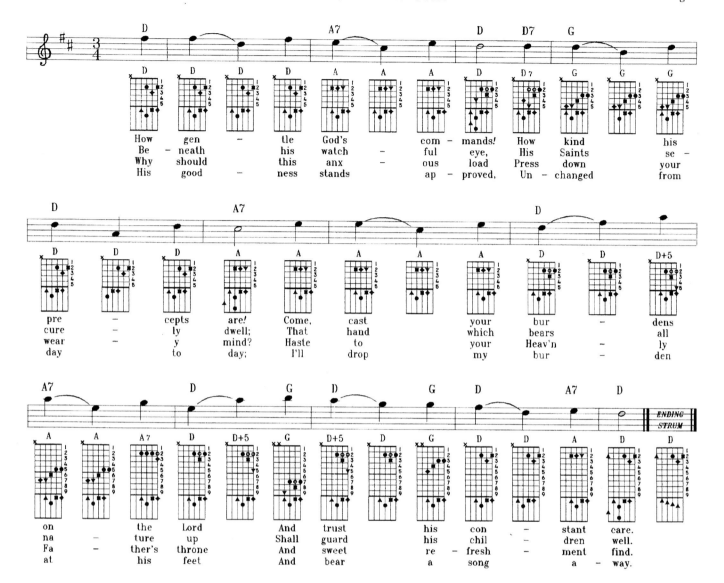

HOW GREAT THE WISDOM AND THE LOVE

Words: E. R. Snow

Kimball GuitarPerfect arr.© 2003

Music: Thomas McIntyre

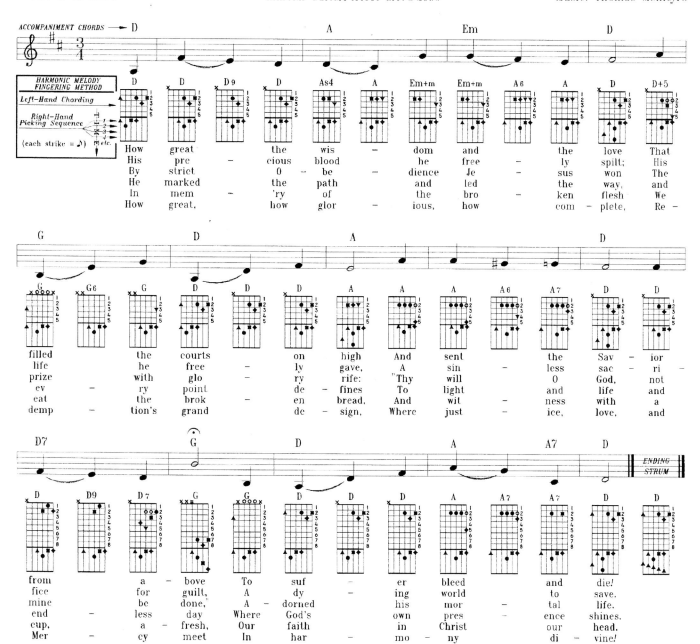

O STORE GUD!

Kimball GuitarPerfect arr.© 2003

Swedish Melody

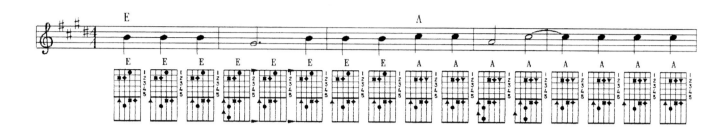

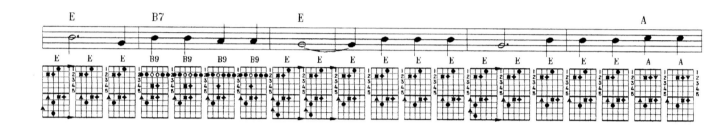

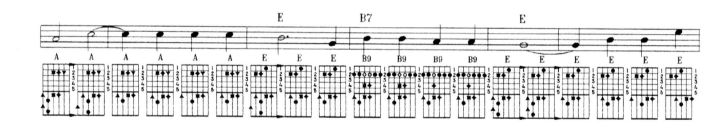

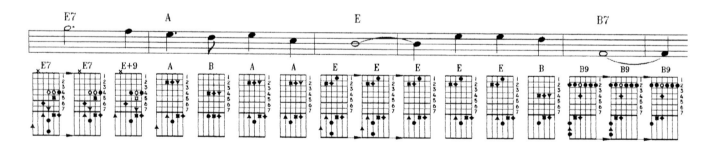

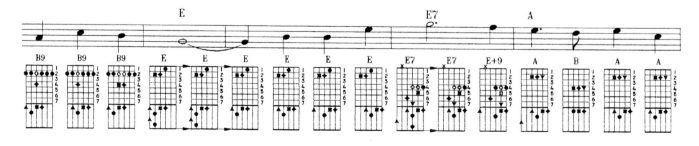

O STORE GUD (cont.)

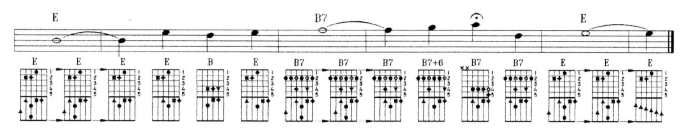

I AM A CHILD OF GOD

Words: Naomi W. Randall

©1998 by Intellectual Reserve, Inc.
Used by Permission
Kimball GuitarPerfect arr. ©2003

Music: Mildred T. Pettit

I KNOW MY FATHER LIVES

Words and Music: R. N. Nibley

Kimball GuitarPerfect arr. ©2003

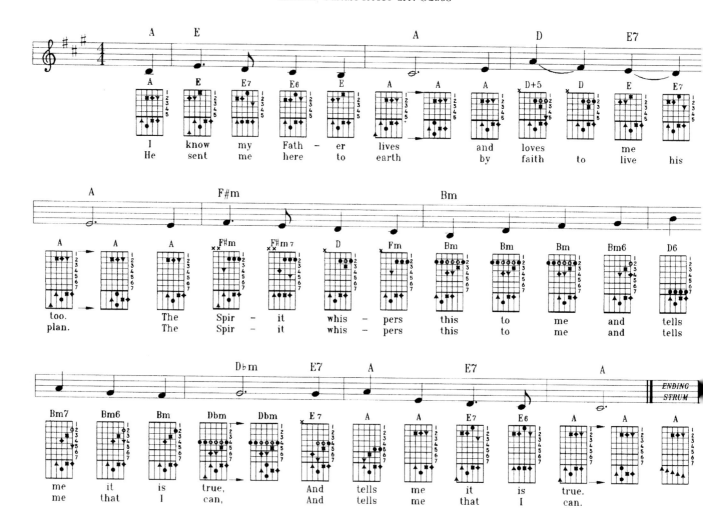

I KNOW THAT MY REDEEMER LIVES

Words: Samuel Medley

Kimball GuitarPerfect arr.© 2003

Music: Lewis D. Edwards

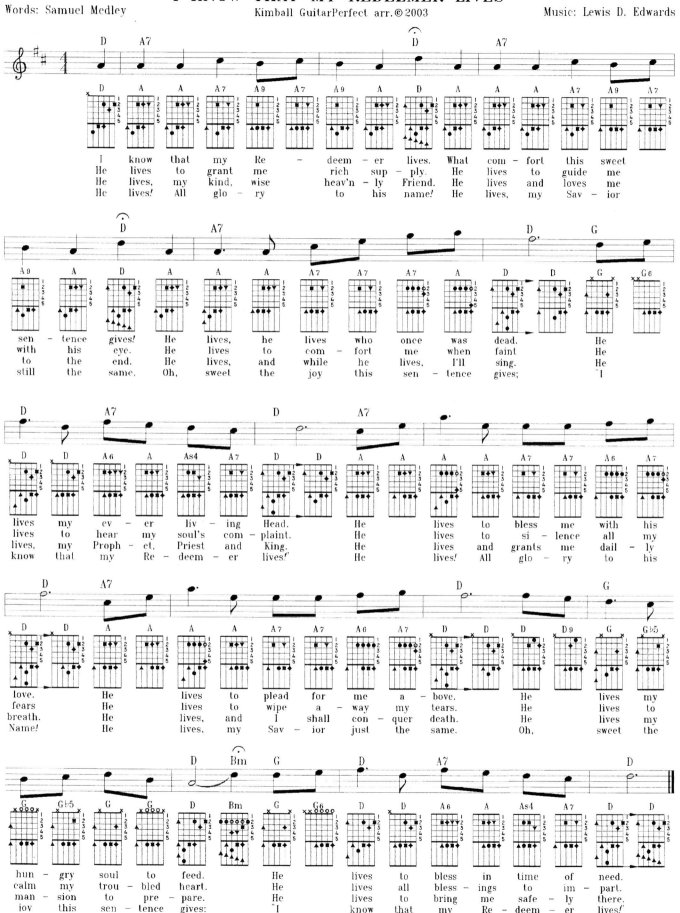

I NEED THEE EVERY HOUR

Kimball GuitarPerfect arr.© 2003

Words: Annie S. Hawkes

Music: Robert Lowry

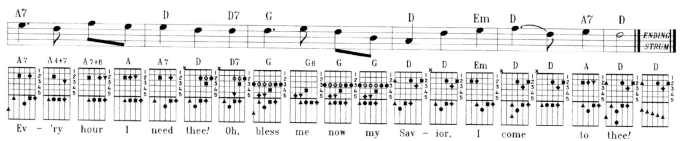

I STAND ALL AMAZED

Words and Music: Charles H. Gabriel

Kimball GuitarPerfect arr.© 2003

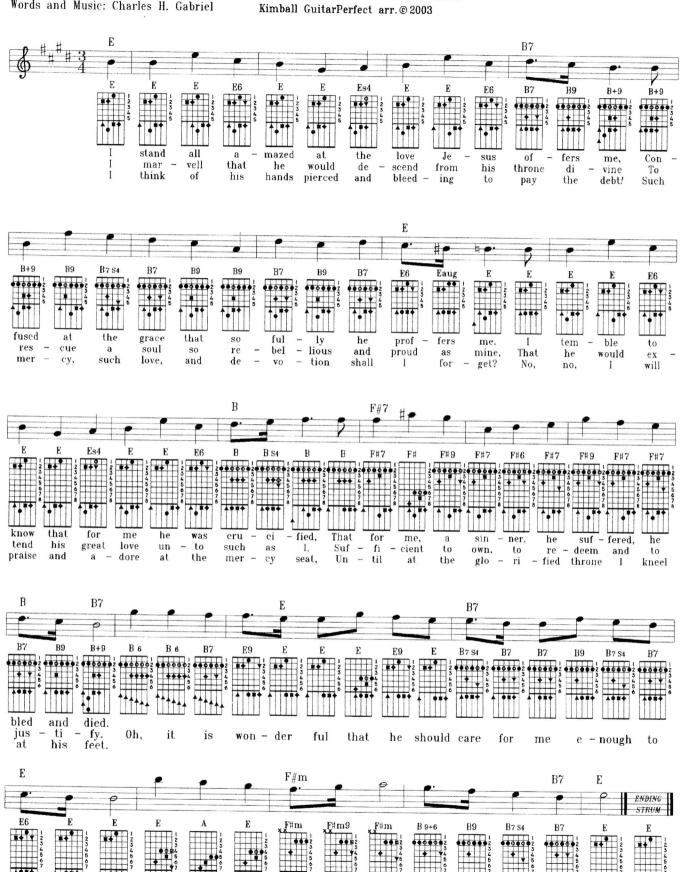

I'LL GO WHERE YOU WANT ME TO GO

Words: Mary Brown

Kimball GuitarPerfect arr.© 2003

Music: Carrie E. Rounsefell

I'LL GO WHERE YOU WANT ME TO GO (cont.)

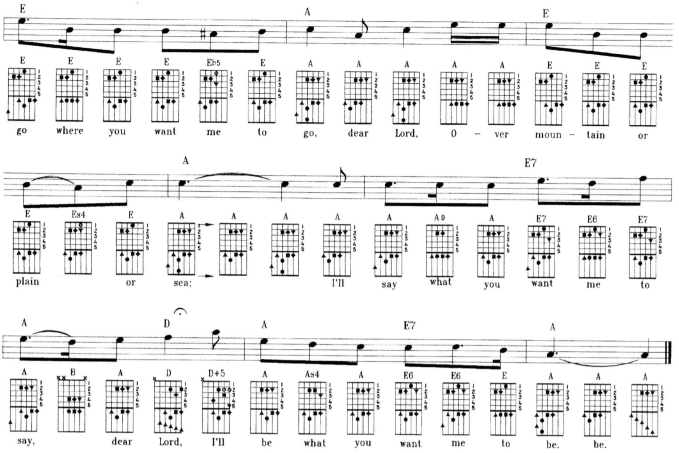

go where you want me to go, dear Lord, O - ver moun - tain or plain or sea; I'll say what you want me to say, dear Lord, I'll be what you want me to be. be.

JESUS, THE VERY THOUGHT OF THEE

Words: Bernard of Clairvaux — Kimball GuitarPerfect arr.© 2003 — Music: John B. Dykes

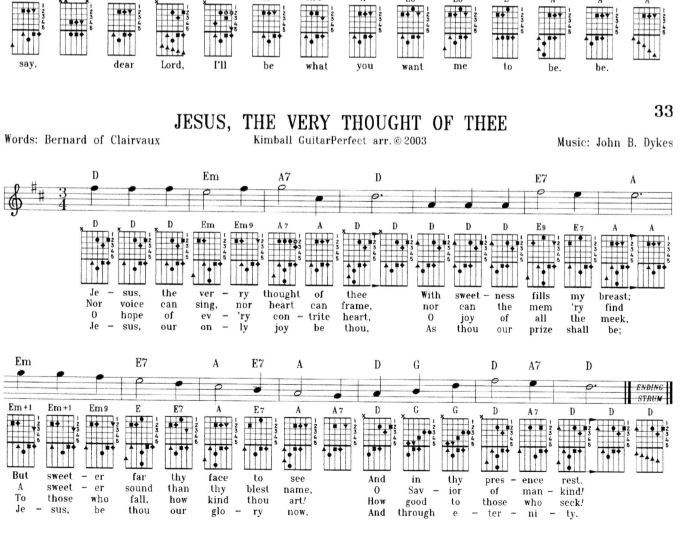

Je - sus, the ver - ry thought of thee With sweet - ness fills my breast;
Nor voice can sing, nor heart can frame, nor can the mem 'ry find
O hope of ev - 'ry con - trite heart, O joy of all the meek,
Je - sus, our on - ly joy be thou, As thou our prize shall be;

But sweet - er far thy face to see And in thy pres - ence rest.
A sweet - er sound than thy kind name, O Sav - ior of man - kind!
To those who fall, how kind thou art! How good to those who seek!
Je - sus, be thou our glo - ry now, And through e - ter - ni - ty.

IN THE GARDEN

Words and Music: C. Austin Miles

Kimball GuitarPerfect arr.©2003

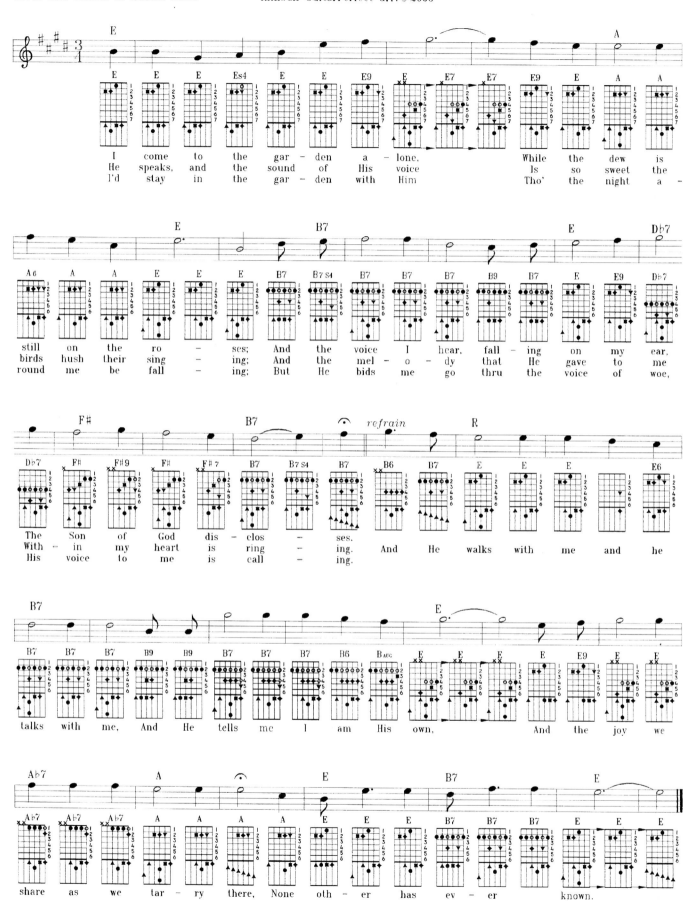

JESUS, SAVIOR, PILOT ME

Words: Edgar Hopper

Kimball GuitarPerfect arr.© 2003

Music: John Edgar Gould

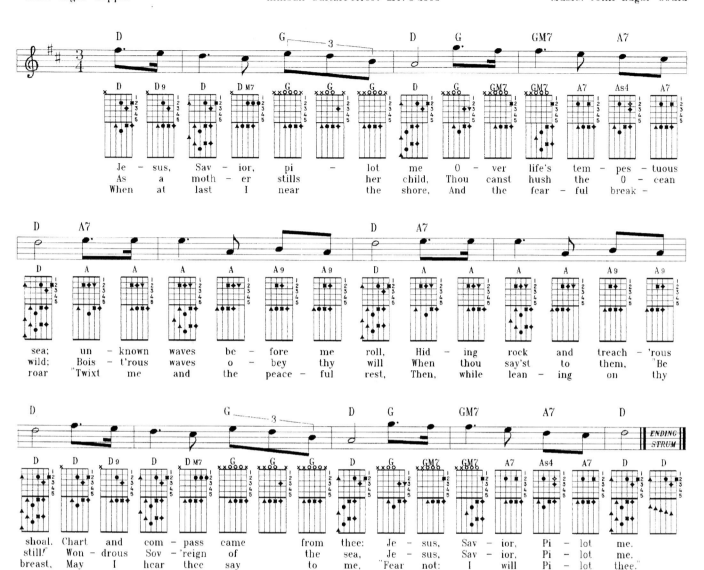

LEAD KINDLY LIGHT

Kimball GuitarPerfect arr. © 2003

Words: John Henry Newman

Music: John B. Dykes

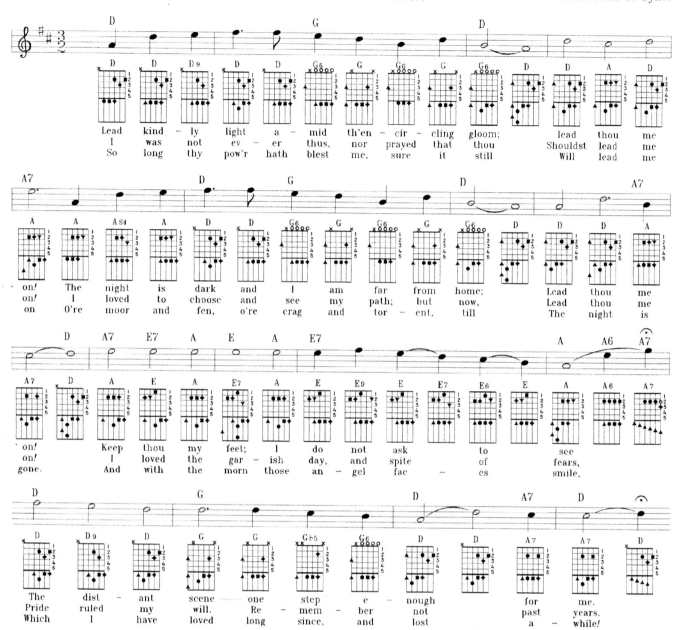

LIGHT OF THE MORNING

Words: C. D. Martin

Kimball GuitarPerfect arr.© 2003

Music: Wm. J. C. Thiel

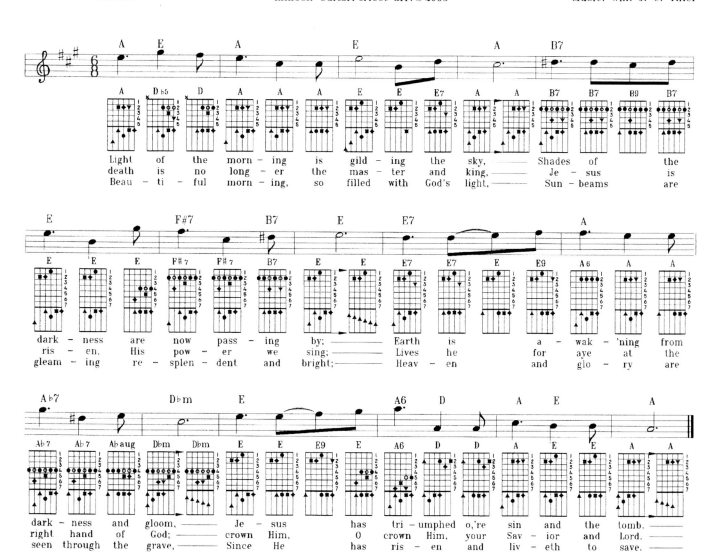

Light of the morn - ing is gild - ing the sky, ____ Shades of the
death is no long - er the mas - ter and king, ____ Je - sus is
Beau - ti - ful morn - ing, so filled with God's light, ____ Sun - beams are

dark - ness are now pass - ing by; ____ Earth is a - wak - 'ning from
ris - en, His pow - er we sing; ____ Lives he for aye at the
gleam - ing re - splen - dent and bright; ____ Heav - en and glo - ry are

dark - ness and gloom, ____ Je - sus has tri - umphed o,'re sin and the tomb. ____
right hand of God; ____ crown Him, O crown Him, your Sav - ior and Lord. ____
seen through the grave, ____ Since He has ris - en and liv - eth to save. ____

LITTLE BROWN CHURCH IN THE VALE

Words and Music: William S. Pitts

Kimball GuitarPerfect arr.© 2003

LOVE AT HOME

Words and Music: John Hugh McNaughton   Kimball GuitarPerfect arr. © 2003

MORE HOLINESS GIVE ME

Words and Music: Philip Paul Bliss

Kimball GuitarPerfect arr.© 2003

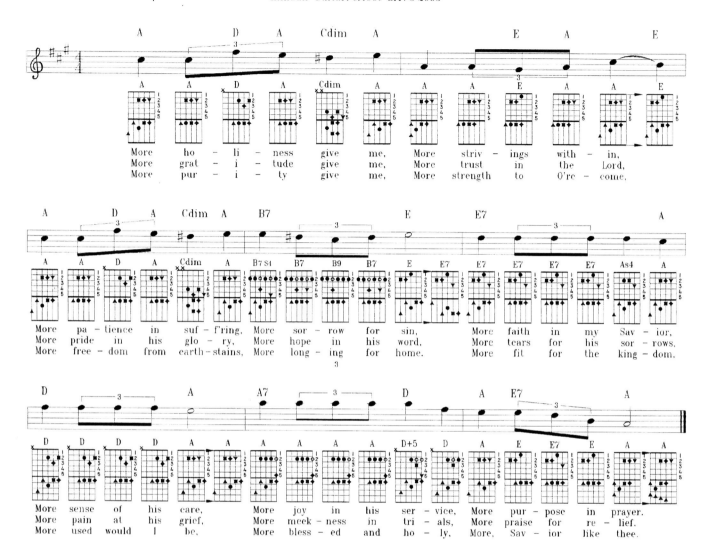

More ho - li - ness give me, More striv - ings with - in,
More grat - i - tude give me, More trust in the Lord,
More pur - i - ty give me, More strength to O're - come.

More pa - tience in suf - f'ring, More sor - row for sin,
More pride in his glo - ry, More hope in his word.
More free - dom from earth - stains, More long - ing for home.

More faith in my Sav - ior,
More tears for his sor - rows,
More fit for the king - dom.

More sense of his care, More joy in his ser - vice, More pur - pose in prayer.
More pain at his grief, More meek - ness in tri - als, More praise for re - lief.
More used would I be, More bless - ed and ho - ly, More, Sav - ior like thee.

NAY, SPEAK NO ILL

Words and Music: Anonymous

Kimball GuitarPerfect arr.© 2003

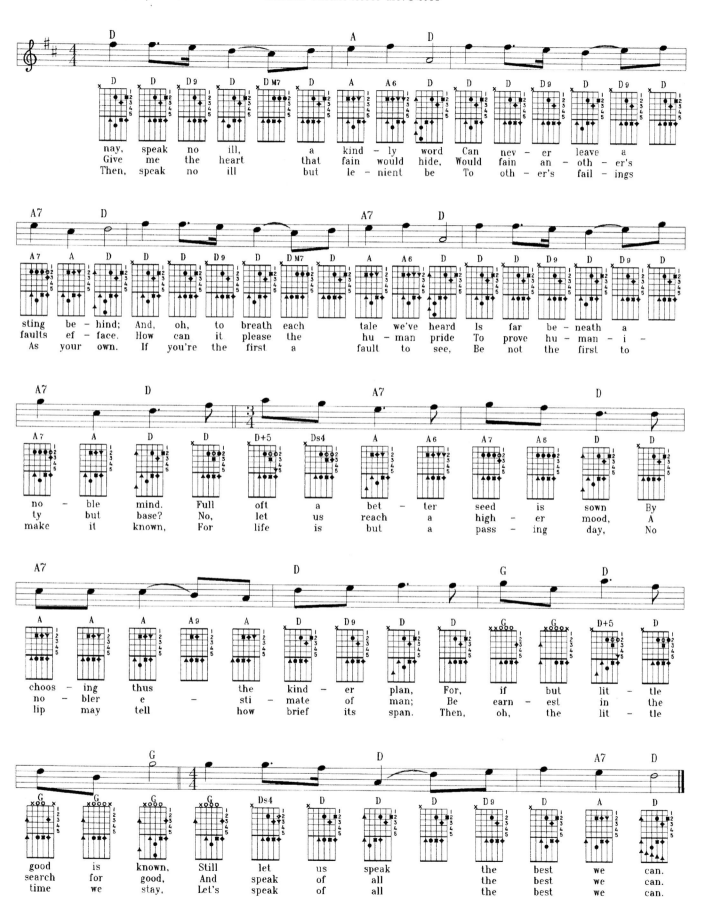

NEARER, MY GOD TO THEE

Words: Sarah F. Adams

Kimball GuitarPerfect arr.© 2003

Music: Lowell Mason

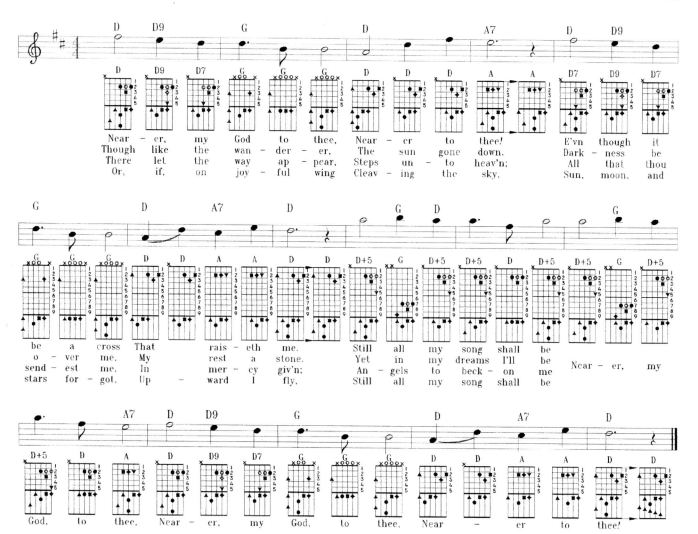

NOW THE DAY IS OVER – Lead

Words: Sabine Baring-Gould

Kimball GuitarPerfect arr.© 2003

Music: Joseph Barnby

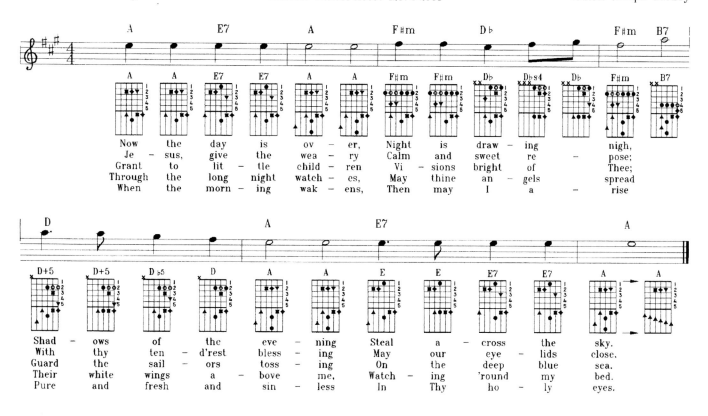

```
Now     the   day   is   ov  –  er,   Night  is   draw – ing      nigh,
Je  –   sus, give  the  wea –  ry   Calm  and  sweet re   –      pose;
Grant   to    lit – tle child – ren   Vi – sions bright of        Thee;
Through the  long  night watch – es,  May  thine  an  – gels      spread
When    the  morn – ing wak –  ens,  Then  may   I   a   –       rise
```

```
Shad  –  ows   of   the   eve  –  ning  Steal  a  –  cross  the   sky.
With     thy   ten – d'rest bless – ing  May  our   eye – lids  close.
Guard    the   sail – ors  toss – ing   On   the   deep  blue  sea.
Their    white wings a  –  bove   me,   Watch – ing 'round my   bed.
Pure     and   fresh and   sin  –  less  In   Thy   ho  – ly   eyes.
```

NOW THE DAY IS OVER – Harmony

Words: Sabine Baring-Gould

Kimball GuitarPerfect arr.© 2003

Music: Joseph Barnby

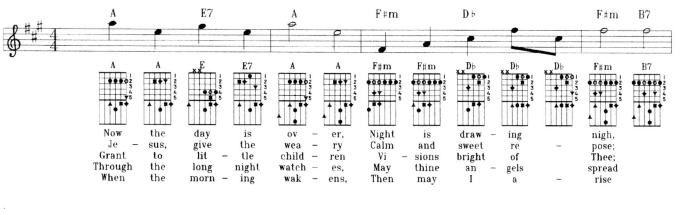

```
Now     the   day   is   ov  –  er,   Night  is   draw – ing      nigh,
Je  –   sus, give  the  wea –  ry   Calm  and  sweet re   –      pose;
Grant   to    lit – tle child – ren   Vi – sions bright of        Thee;
Through the  long  night watch – es,  May  thine  an  – gels      spread
When    the  morn – ing wak –  ens,  Then  may   I   a   –       rise
```

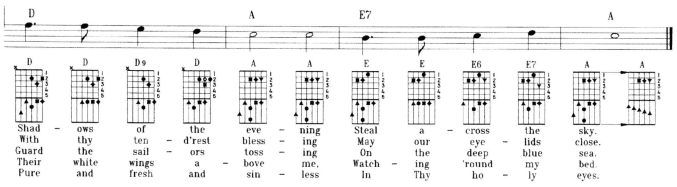

```
Shad  –  ows   of   the   eve  –  ning  Steal  a  –  cross  the   sky.
With     thy   ten – d'rest bless – ing  May  our   eye – lids  close.
Guard    the   sail – ors  toss – ing   On   the   deep  blue  sea.
Their    white wings a  –  bove   me,   Watch – ing 'round my   bed.
Pure     and   fresh and   sin  –  less  In   Thy   ho  – ly   eyes.
```

ONWARD, CHRISTIAN SOLDIERS

Words: Sabine Baring-Gould

Kimball GuitarPerfect arr.© 2003

Music: Arthur S. Sullivan

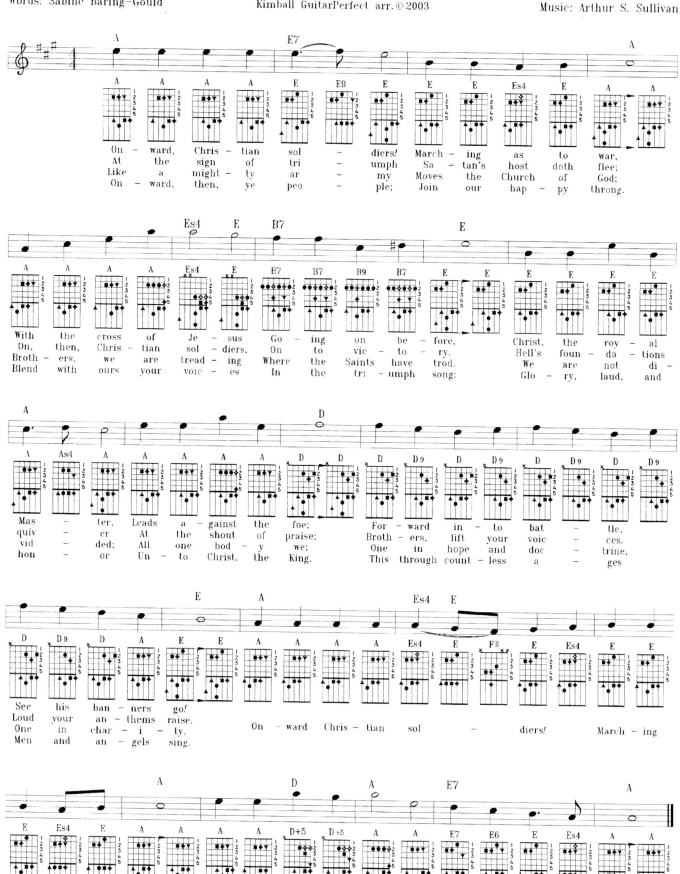

PRAYER IS THE SOUL'S SINCERE DESIRE

Words: James Montgomery

Kimball GuitarPerfect arr.© 2003

Music: George Careless

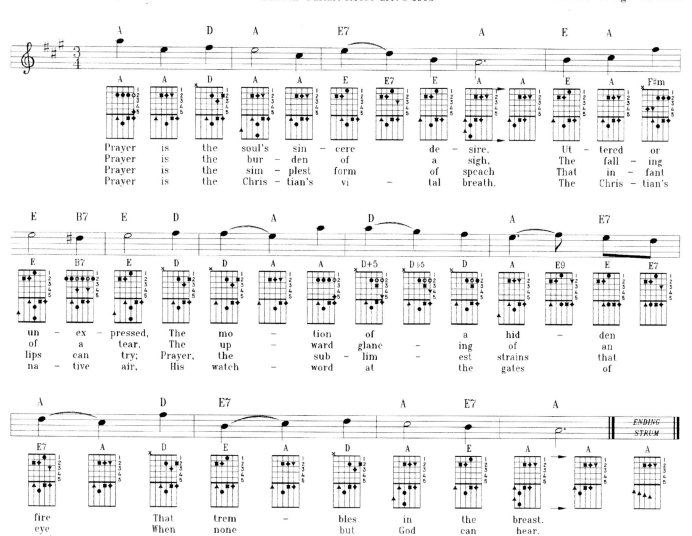

Prayer is the soul's sin - cere de - sire, Ut - tered or
Prayer is the bur - den of a sigh, The fall - ing
Prayer is the sim - plest form of speach That in - fant
Prayer is the Chris - tian's vi - tal breath, The Chris - tian's

un - ex - pressed, The mo - tion of a hid - den
of a can - try; The up - ward glanc - ing of an
lips na - tive air, His watch - word sub - lim - est strains that
na - tive air, His watch - word at the gates of

fire That trem - bles in the breast.
eye When none but God can hear.
reach The maj - es - ty on high.
death; He en - ters heav'n with prayer.

ENDING
STRUM

PRECIOUS MEMORIES

Words and Music: J. B. F. Wright

Kimball GuitarPerfect arr.© 2003

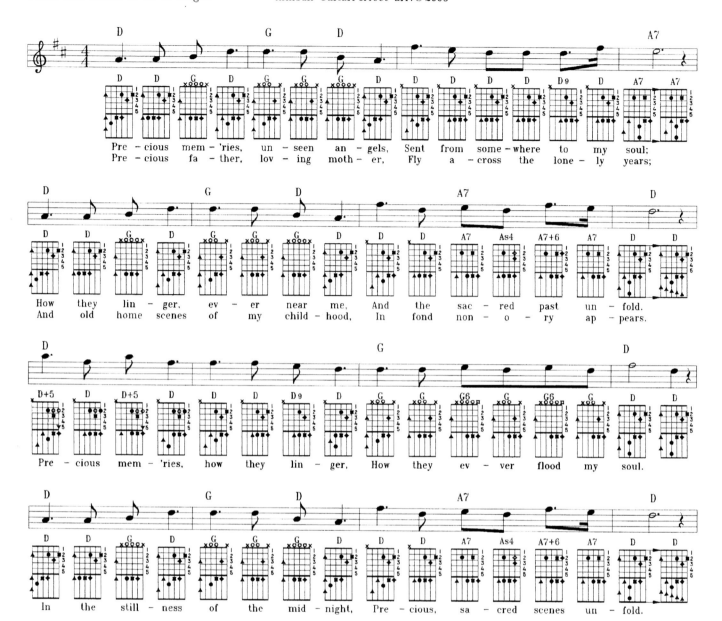

ROCK OF AGES

Words: August M. Toplady

Kimball GuitarPerfect arr. © 2003

Music: Thomas Hastings

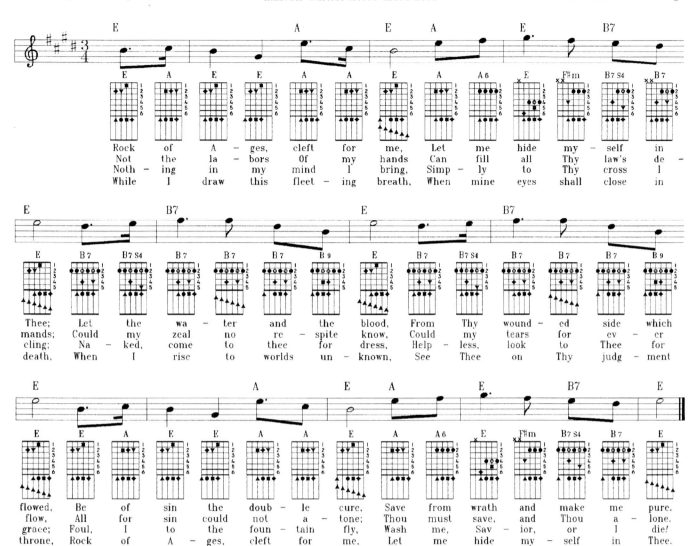

Rock of A – ges, cleft for me, Let me hide my – self in
Not the la – bors Of my hands Can fill all Thy law's de –
Noth – ing la in my mind I bring, Simp – ly to Thy cross I
While I draw this fleet – ing breath, When mine eyes shall close in

Thee; Let the wa – ter and the blood, From Thy wound – ed side which
mands; Could my zeal no re – spite know, Could my tears for ev – er
cling; Na – ked, come to thee for dress, Help – less, look to Thee for
death, When I rise to worlds un – known, See Thee on Thy judg – ment

flowed, Be of sin the doub – le cure, Save from wrath and make me pure.
flow, All for sin could not a – tone; Thou must save, and Thou a – lone.
grace; Foul, I to the foun – tain fly, Wash me, Sav – ior, or I die!
throne, Rock of A – ges, cleft for me, Let me hide my – self in Thee.

REVERENTLY AND MEEKLY NOW

Words: Joseph L. Townsend
Kimball GuitarPerfect arr.©2003
Music: Ebenezer Beesley

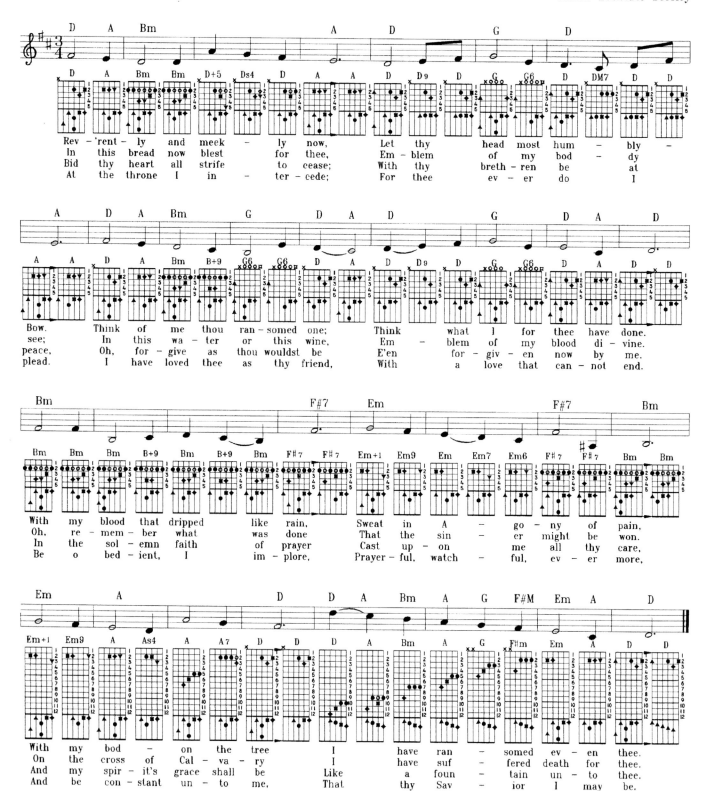

SECRET PRAYER

Words and music: Hans Henry Petersen

Kimball GuitarPerfect arr.© 2003

SHALL WE GATHER AT THE RIVER?

Words: Robert Lowry

Kimball GuitarPerfect arr.© 2003

Music: Robert Lowry

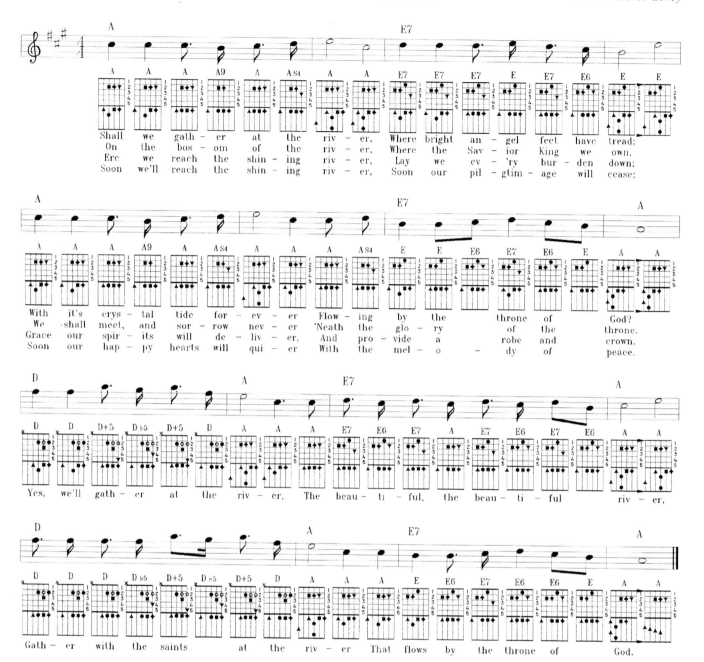

SOFTY AND TENDERLY

Words and Music: Will L. Thompson

Kimball GuitarPerfect arr. © 2003

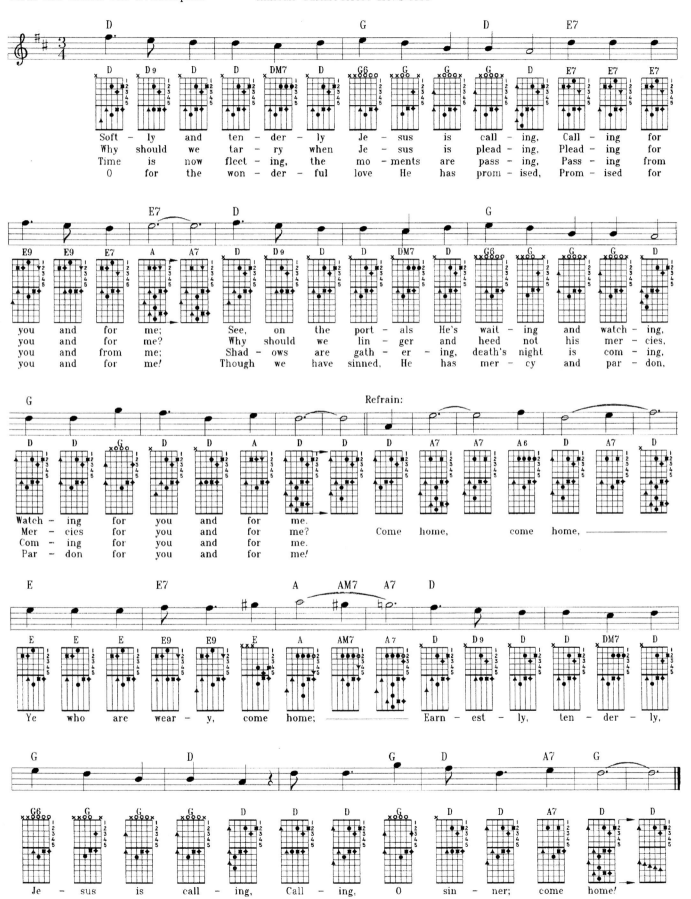

SWEET HOUR OF PRAYER

Words: William W. Walford

Kimball GuitarPerfect arr. © 2003

Music: William B. Bradbury

Sweet / Sweet hour / hour of / of prayer! / prayer! Sweet / Sweet hour / hour of / of prayer! / prayer! That / Thy calls / wings me / shall from / my a pe-

world / ti of / tion care / bear And / To bids / him me / whose at / truth my / and Fa- / faith ther's / full throne- / ness Make / En all / gage my / the

wants / wait and / ing wish / soul es / to known. / bless. In / And sea- / since sons / he of / bids dis- / me tress / seek and / his grief, / face, My / Be

soul / lieve has / his of / word ten / and found / trust re- / his lief / grace, And / I'll oft / cast es- / on caped / him the / my temp- / ev ter's / 'ry

snare / care, By / And thy / wait re- / for turn, / thee, sweet / sweet hour / hour of / of prayer! / prayer! And / I'll oft / cast es- / on

caped / him the / my temp- / ev er's / 'ry snare / care, by / And thy / wait re- / for turn, / thee, sweet / sweet hour / hour of / of prayer! / prayer!

SWEET IS THE WORK

Words: Isaac Watts

Kimball GuitarPerfect arr. © 2003

Music: John J. McClellan

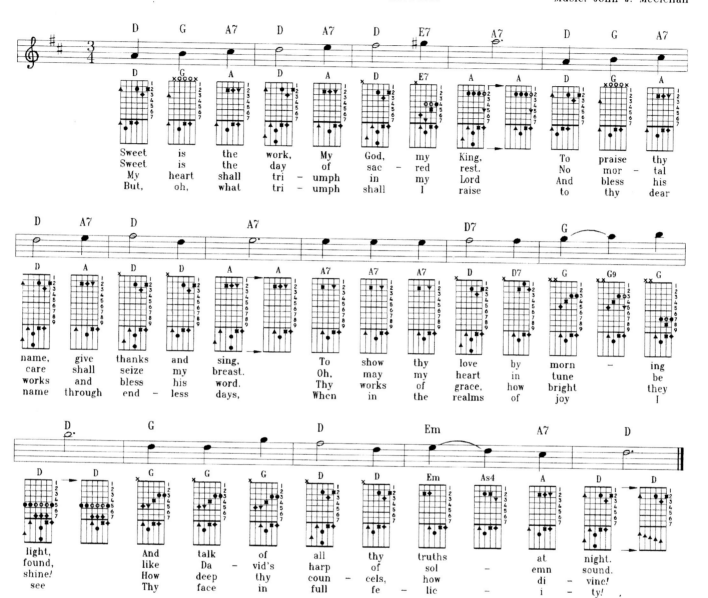

THE LORD IS MY SHEPHERD – Lead

Words: James Montgomery

Kimball GuitarPerfect arr.©2003

Music: Thomas Koschat

THE LORD IS MY SHEPHERD – Harmony

Words: James Montgomery

Kimball GuitarPerfect arr. © 2003

Music: Thomas Koschat

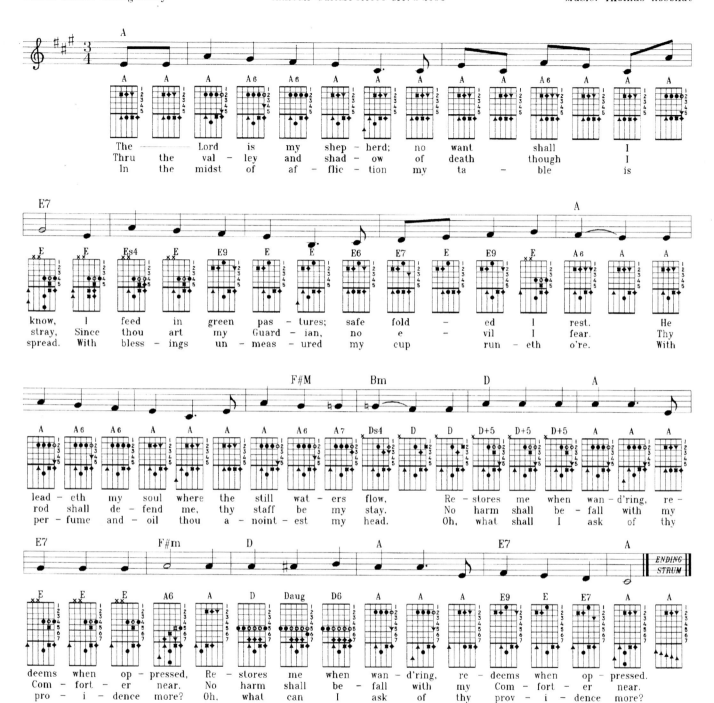

THE OLD RUGGED CROSS

Words and Music: George Bennard

Kimball GuitarPerfect arr.© 2003

THERE IS A GREEN HILL FAR AWAY

Words: Cecil Frances Alexander

Kimball GuitarPerfect arr.© 2003

Music: John H. Gower

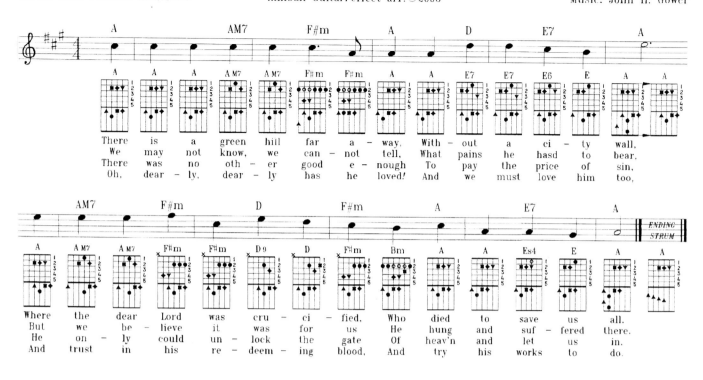

There is a green hill far — a — way, With — out a ci — ty wall,
We may not know, we can — not tell, What pains he hasd to bear,
There was no oth — er good e — nough To pay the price of sin,
Oh, dear — ly, dear — ly has he loved! And we must love him too,

Where the dear Lord was cru — ci — fied. Who died to save us all.
But we on — ly be — lieve it could un — lock the gate Of heav'n and let us in.
He on — ly trust in his re — deem — ing blood, And try his works to do.
And

PRAISE GOD FROM WHOM ALL BLESSINGS FLOW

Words: Thomas Ken

Kimball GuitarPerfect arr.© 2003

Music: Louis Bourgeous

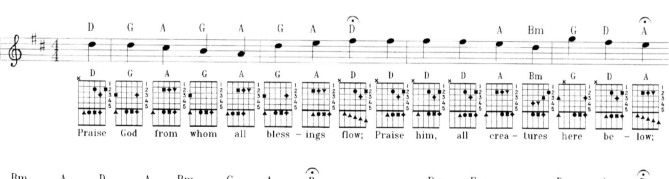

Praise God from whom all bless — ings flow; Praise him, all crea — tures here be — low;

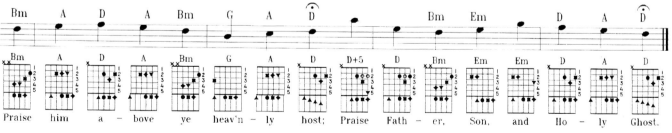

Praise him a — bove ye heav'n — ly host; Praise Fath — er, Son, and Ho — ly Ghost.

THOUGH DEEPENING TRIALS

Kimball GuitarPerfect arr.© 2003

Words: E. R. Snow

Music: George Careless

WERE YOU THERE?

Words and Music: Traditional Spiritual

Kimball GuitarPerfect arr. © 2003

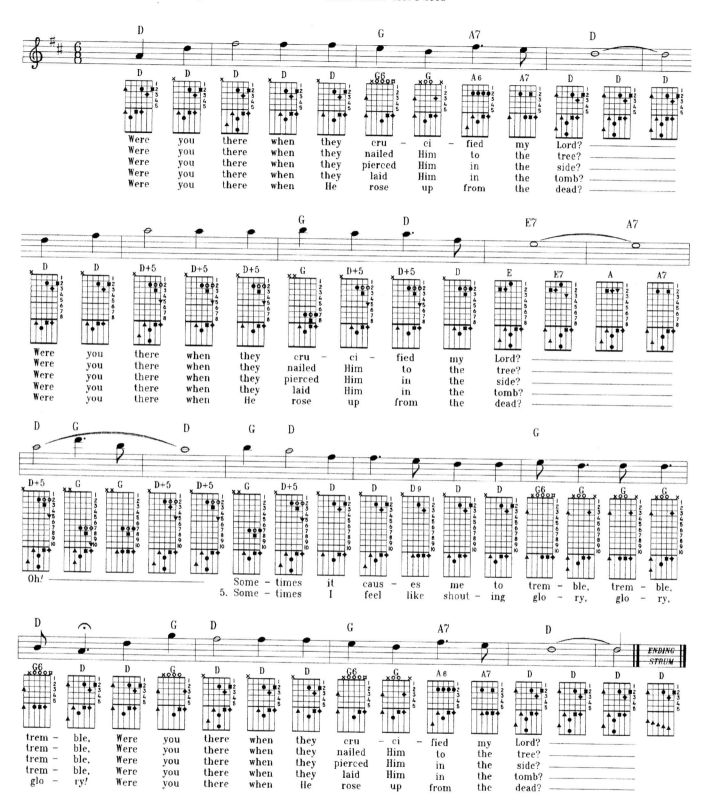

WHAT A FRIEND WE HAVE IN JESUS

Words: Joseph Scriven

Kimball GuitarPerfect arr.© 2003

Music: Charles C. Converse

What _ a friend _ we have in Je = sus,
Have we trials and temp – ta –tions?
Are we weak and heav – y la – den,

All _ our sins and griefs to bear!
Is there troub – le an – y whaere?
Cum –bered with a load of care?

What a priv – i – ledge to car – ry
We should nev – er be dis – cour – aged,
Pre – cious Sav – ior, still our re – fuge;

Ev – 'ry thing to God in prayer!
Take it to the Lord in prayer;
Take it to the Lord in prayer;

Oh, what peace we of – ten for – feit,
Can we find a friend so faith – ful,
Do thy find friends de – spise, for – sake thee?

Oh, what need – less pain we bear,
Who will all our sor – rows share?
Take it to the Lord in prayer;

All be – cause we do not car – ry
Je – sus knows our ver – y weak – ness,
In His arms He'll take and shield thee;

Ev – ry thing to god in prayer!
Take it to the Lord in prayer.
Thou wilt find a sol – ace there.

WHAT A FRIEND WE HAVE IN JESUS

Words: Joseph Scriven

Kimball GuitarPerfect arr.©2003

Music: Charles C. Converse

WHISPERING HOPE

Words and Music: Alice Hawthorne

Kimball GuitarPerfect arr.© 2003

WHISPERING HOPE (cont.)

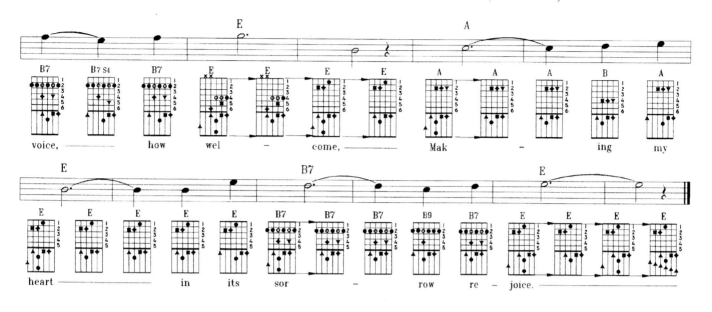

voice, ———— how wel – come, ———— Mak – ing my

heart ———— in its sor – row re – joice.

UPON THE CROSS OF CALVARY

Words: Vilate Raile   Kimball GuitarPerfect arr.© 2003   Music: Leroy Robertson

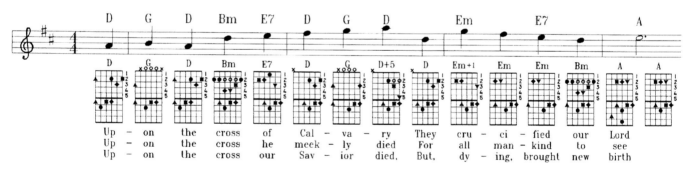

Up – on the cross of Cal – va – ry They cru – ci – fied our Lord
Up – on the cross he meek – ly died For all man – kind to see
Up – on the cross our Sav – ior died, But, dy – ing, brought new birth

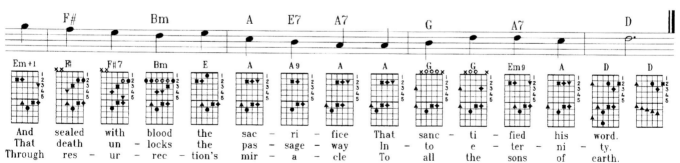

And sealed with blood the sac – ri – fice That sanc – ti – fied his word.
That death un – locks the pas – sage – way In – to e – ter – ni – ty.
Through res – ur – rec – tion's mir – a – cle To all the sons of earth.

Christmas Songs

AWAY IN A MANGER

Words: Anonymous   Kimball GuitarPerfect arr.© 2003   Music: William J. Kirkpatrick

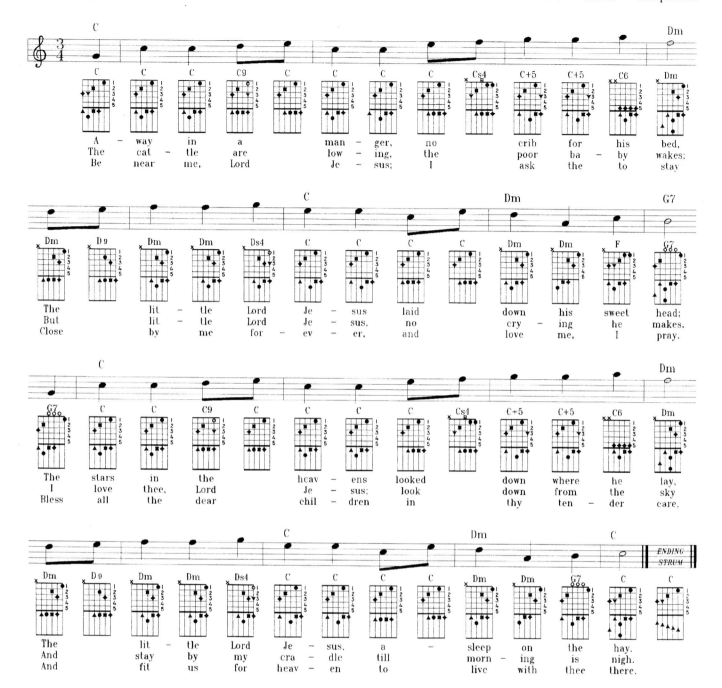

I HEARD THE BELLS ON CHRISTMAS DAY

Words: Henry Wadsworth Longfellow   Kimball GuitarPerfect arr.© 2003   Music: John Baptiste Calkin

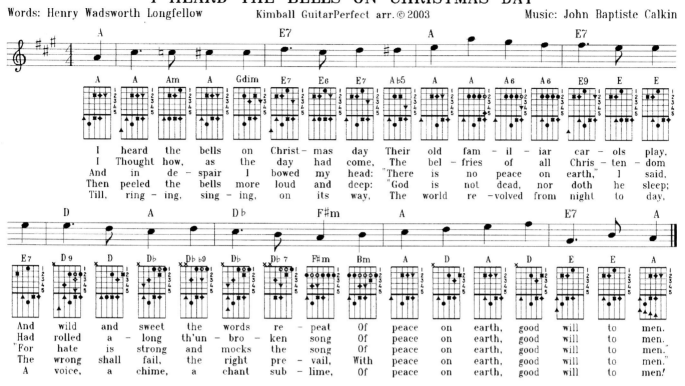

I	heard	the	bells	on	Christ-	mas	day	Their	old	fam	-	il	iar	car	-	ols	play.
I	Thought	how,	as	the	day-	had	come,	The	bel	-	fries	of	all	Chris	-	ten	dom
And	in	de	-	spair	I	bowed	my	head:	"There	is	no	peace	on	earth,"	I	said,
Then	peeled	the	bells	more	loud	and	deep:	"God	is	not	dead,	nor	doth	he	sleep;
Till,	ring	-	ing,	sing	-	ing,	on	its	way,	The	world	re	-volved	from	night	to	day,

And	wild	and	sweet	the	words	re	-	peat	Of	peace	on	earth,	good	will	to	men.
Had	rolled	a	-	long	th'un	-	bro	-	ken	song	Of	peace	on	earth,	good	will	to	men.
"For	hate	is	strong	and	mocks	the	song	Of	peace	on	earth,	good	will	to	men."
The	wrong	shall	fail,	the	right	pre	-	vail,	With	peace	on	earth,	good	will	to	men."
A	voice,	a	chime,	a	chant	sub	-	lime,	Of	peace	on	earth,	good	will	to	men!

FAR, FAR AWAY ON JUDEA'S PLAINS

Words and Music: John Menzies Macfarlane   Kimball GuitarPerfect arr.© 2003

Far,	far	a	-	way	on	Ju	-	de	-	a's	plains,	Shep	-	herds	of	old	heard	the
Sweet	are	these	strains	of	re	-	deem	-	ing	love,	mes	-	sage	of	mer	-	cy	from
Lord,	with	the	an	-	gels	we	too	would	re	-	joice;	Help	us	to	sing	with	the
Has	-	ten	the	time	when	from	ev	-	'ry	clime,	Men	shall	u	-	nite	in	the

joy	-	ous	strains:
heav'n	a	-	bove:
heart	and	voice:
strains	sub	-	lime:

Glo - ry to god, glo - ry to God, Glo - ry to God in the

high - est; Peace on earth, good will to men; Peace on earth, good will to men!

IT CAME UPON A MIDNIGHT CLEAR

Words: Edmund H. Sears

Kimball GuitarPerfect arr.© 2003

Music: Richard S. Willis

OH, COME ALL YE FAITHFUL

Words: Attr. to John F. Wade
Trans. by Frederick Oakeley

Kimball GuitarPerfect arr.© 2003

Music: attr. to John F. Wade

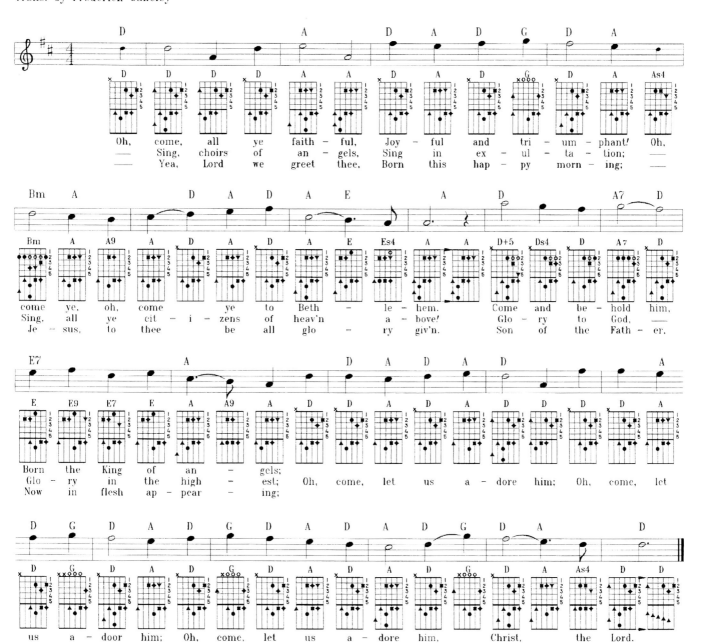

O COME, O COME, EMMANUEL

Kimball GuitarPerfect arr. ©2003

Words: Latin Hymn
Trans. by John M Neale

Music: Thomas Helmore

SILENT NIGHT

Kimball GuitarPerfect arr. © 2003

Words: Joseph Mohr

Music: Franz Gruber

WITH WONDERING AWE

Words and Music: Anonymous
From: Laudis Corona, Boston

Kimball GuitarPerfect arr.© 2003

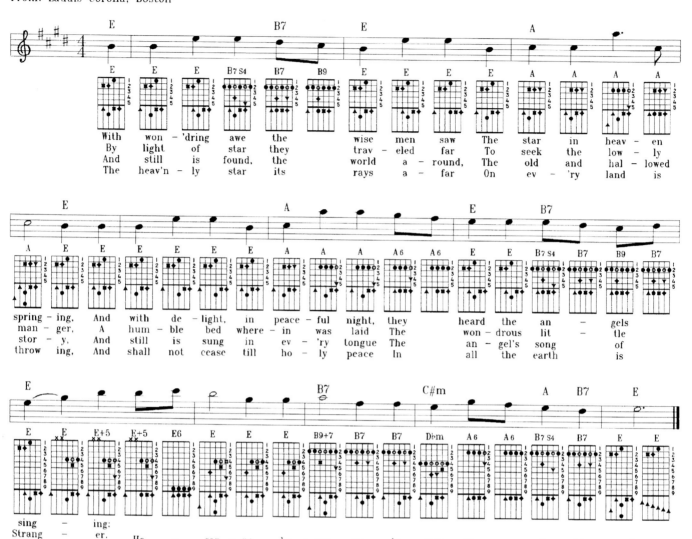

WHAT CHILD IS THIS?

Text: William C. Dix

Kimball GuitarPerfect arr.© 2003

English Melody

WHAT CHILD IS THIS?

Words: William C. Dix

Kimball GuitarPerfect, arr.© 2003

English Melody

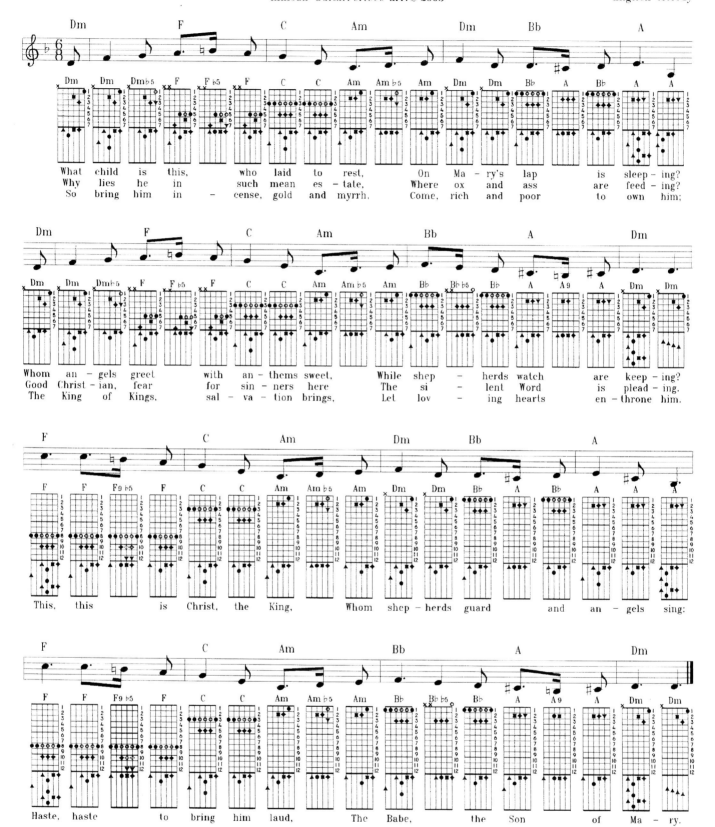

What child is this, who laid to rest, On Ma - ry's lap is sleep - ing?
Why lies he in such mean es - tate, Where ox and ass are feed - ing?
So bring him in - cense, gold and myrrh, Come, rich and poor to own him;

Whom an - gels greet with an - thems sweet, While shep - herds watch are keep - ing?
Good Christ - ian, fear for sin - ners here The si - lent Word is plead - ing.
The King of Kings, sal - va - tion brings, Let lov - ing hearts en - throne him.

This, this is Christ, the King, Whom shep - herds guard and an - gels sing:

Haste, haste to bring him laud, The Babe, the Son of Ma - ry.